BOMBAY

PLACE-NAMES AND STREET-NAMES

*An excursion into the by-ways of
the history of Bombay city*

BOMBAY

PLACE-NAMES AND STREET-NAMES

An excursion into the by-ways of
the history of Bombay city

Samuel T. Sheppard

Foreword by Sidharth Bhatia

Indus Source Books

Indian Spirit, Universal Wisdom

Indus Source Books
PO Box 6194
Malabar Hill PO
Mumbai 400 006
INDIA
Email: info@indussource.com
www.indussource.com

Bombay Place-Names and Street-Names

ISBN: 978-93-85509-41-4

Originally published as *Bombay Place-Names and Street-Names*
by Samuel T. Sheppard, Times Press, Bombay, 1917

Cover design Sanskruti Graphics, Mumbai.

Printed at Thomson Press India Ltd., New Delhi.

Contents

Foreword   vi

Preface   xi

Bombay Place-Names   1

Notes   168

Foreword

FOR true Bombay history buffs, Samuel T. Sheppard's classic *Bombay Place-Names and Street-Names*, is a much-loved book. The sub-title of the book, *An excursion into the by-ways of the history of Bombay city*, says it all: it is not just an exploration of the names but also the colourful local histories of the streets, bringing to life many intricate details about the entire area.

That it was written in 1917, when the city was on the cusp of another great change – the development of the "northern" areas of Dadar and Matunga and the grand reclamation of the sea on the west from Chowpatty, or Backbay, that would become Marine Drive — adds to the flavour and nostalgia. It is a book to read and savour, as one walks around, exploring the city.

Walking down a city street is one of the joys of modern life. To the aimless wanderer, the *flaneur*, to use a colourful French word, a street yields many secrets and surprises, its buildings, shops and nooks and crannies full of tales of other times. Many questions arise as one ambles — Who lives in those buildings? Who set up that restaurant? Does that small tailor have clients anymore? And, most of all, who is the street named after?

Different cities around the world have followed different policies when it comes to naming their streets. In New York, for example, the grid system divides the city into avenues and side streets. While the broader avenues, which cut across the city north to south, are named, the streets are numbered. In Britain, it is common to find a Main Street or King's Road almost everywhere, but confusion arises when one is confronted with a

Road or Crescent with the same name.

Closer home, Delhi's wide boulevards are named after the grand Mughals (Akbar, Humayun), after more contemporary cultural figures (Amrita Shergil) and after international leaders (Tito, Makarios). Cleverly, the diplomatic quarter, where most of the foreign missions are, has names like Chanakyapuri, Niti Marg and Shanti Path.

The inner streets are another story. As the city spread outwards from the 1950s onwards, many residential enclaves — called colonies — were built and each segment was called a "block", with numbered plots. Thus, a house is identified not by its name but by a complex set of hieroglyphics such as A/89/1, which to an outsider looks like a bureaucrat's mystifying notings on a file but which a local decodes immediately.

In contrast, most of the streets in Mumbai, big or small, are named — after people, local landmarks, towns, local fauna and even occupations. As a much younger city, which was founded by British colonialists Mumbai — then Bombay — was sparsely populated, with a few scattered communities whose main activity was farming, fishing or toddy tapping.

What the British got was several small islands separated by water and swamps. In time, these were reclaimed and the islands linked with each other. The construction of infrastructure and the creation of key institutions followed and by the end of the eighteenth century, Bombay had the makings of a town. The mid-nineteenth century saw rapid development and in 1888, with the formation of the Bombay Municipal Corporation, a proper governing body for the city was created.

It can be presumed that the formal task of naming streets began then. As Sheppard writes in this wonderful book, "It is remarkable that the scheme for a statistical account of Bombay quoted as an appendix to Vol I of the late Sir J.M. Campbell's 'Bombay Town and Island Materials,' (1894), while proposing the collection of many details about the roads, makes no allusion to the names of roads. Under the heading of Bridges, however, in that scheme 'name and origin of the name' are included among other points of interest to be discovered, and in the more recent Gazetteer of Bombay City and Island, by Mr. S.M. Edwardes, (1909) considerable attention has been paid to the general subject of names."

From these we can conclude that till the late nineteenth century the streets had no names, though of course traditional names for localities existed from much earlier. Bombay's neighbourhoods were often named after reigning goddesses and some names are in use even today — Prabhadevi, Sitladevi, Mumbadevi are good examples. Names such as Worli or Parel (spelt in old maps as Worlee and Parell) have a hoary past too.

By the time Sheppard published his book, most if not all streets of Bombay — which ended at Mahim on the one side and Sion on the other — had proper names, though urban development had not reached beyond Parel. It was only around that time that roads and habitats were being constructed under the banner of the Bombay Improvement Trust in Dadar, Matunga, King's Circle and Sion. How well those areas were planned is apparent to this day.

Some stretches, such as Hornby Vellard, which links Mahalakshmi to Worli, and was the earliest example of reclamation, was called that after the engineer who built it, as was Bellassis Road (from Parel Road to Bellasis Bridge), which was built in 1793 under the orders of Major General Bellasis. However, Sheppard doesn't say whether these were named then or later.

There is a general impression that the British administrators of the city chose to name everything — streets, avenues, bridges and railway stations — after either the British monarchy or colonial officials. Victoria Terminus or the Prince of Wales Museum are cited as examples. Sandhurst Road, Grant Road, Frere Road are named after important British governors and administrators.

But this is not the whole truth. Going through this book, it becomes clear that there were many streets, alleys and even thoroughfares that were named after local Indian notables. Some of them are in use even today. The very first name in the book's listing is Abdul Rehman Street (from Crawford Market to Pydhonie), which was apparently named after a Konkani Muslim who owned a lot of land in the neighbourhood.

Nor was there any over-emphasis on any one community. Hindus, Muslims, Christians, Jews and of course Parsis, are all represented. How diverse the city was even then is obvious from names such as Arab Lane, Armenian Lane, Israel Mohalla and Chini Gully.

Some names are reflective of the vast areas under what was known as Bombay Presidency. The Bombay Port Trust, which handled goods from all over the western and southern region named its streets after coastal towns and locations — thus, even today, there are streets called Goa, Karwar, Cochin, Mangalore and closer places like Kurla and even Bhandup, then a village in north Bombay.

Species of trees find mention too — Ash Lane and Tamarind Lane are small streets that cut across from the aptly named Medows street though the latter refers to Gen. Medows, the governor of Bombay.

Besides the fascinating history behind the names, the book also tells us a lot of about what Bombay was at the time — its communities, its flora, its important British functionaries and Indian grandees and the "celebrities" of the time (usually well-known businessmen or property-owners). Those who owned land inevitably left their imprint on their neighbourhoods. The various numbered Bhoiwada Lanes in Bhuleshwar were named after "Bhois (palanquin bearers) who inhabited the place". The land was "Fazandari tenure" (a form of lease-holding) and the original Fazandars were the Javles, Sheppard informs us.

Bhoiwada, like many other places is still around with its original name intact, as are many other precincts. But several others have been renamed, initially in the first flush after independence and since then under pressure from local residents and influential people, who get the support of politicians.

But old habits die hard. Citizens don't switch to the new names easily. Peddar Road, Nepean Sea Road or Bhatia Baug continue to be referred to by their old names. Most interesting is the case of Hughes Road, which has been renamed but remains, and will remain, Hugis Road for all time to come. (This is not new. As far back as in 1911, *The Times of India* bemoaned the "melancholy example of Hughes Road which some have already converted to Hugis Road.")

Such gems enhance the joys of reading this book. In examining the histories of the names, Sheppard refers to many other published sources providing the reader with so many new reference points to read up on the history of Bombay/Mumbai.

Since original copies of the book are difficult to obtain, the only way to read this book so far was to download it from the Internet. But this fresh new reprint makes it accessible to a whole new generation of readers who want to know more about the great city they live in.

— Sidharth Bhatia

Preface

THIS little book has been many years in preparation and is at last published only because no one else appears to have devoted sufficient time and attention to a subject of which only the fringe has here been touched and which seems to me to be of interest and some importance. A book of this kind ought really to be published only after prolonged research into old leases and deeds. That is beyond my powers but I have none the less thought my less recondite work may be of service. It has steadily grown in scope since I started it as an inquiry into the reason why various English surnames have been given to Bombay roads, but the development has only been possible with the assistance of many gentlemen who have the gift of tongues which has been denied to the author-compiler.

Among the many friends whom I have to thank for valued assistance are the Ho n. Mr. P. R. Cadell, Mr. S. M. Edwardes (from whose writings also I have freely stolen), Mr. J. P. Orr, the Rev. E. R. Hull , S.J. , Mr. R. P. Karkaria , Dr . Jivanji Jamshedji Modi, Mr. R. P. Masani, Rao Bahadur P. B. Joshi, and Mr. Kaikhushro o Pesto nji Bhedwar. Mr. Karkaria in particular has been of great assistance to me and has taken the trouble to visit many streets where the origin of the names was doubtful. The method followed needs some explanation. When only one theory is put forward to account for the origin of a name I have not as a rule stated from whom that theory has been obtained, and by this means, if I appear to gain the credit for many ingenious derivations, I can also bear the blame for any grievous faults that may have crept in. When my authorities have conflicted I have usually stated who they are, and the public which pays its money for the book may take its choice as to which derivation is likely to be the more correct. If any family history has been misrepresented I offer my apologies in advance to any who may feel hurt, for I have not willfully put down anything intended to reflect on anyone' s ancestry or history.

— S. T. S.

Bombay Place-Names

IT is remarkable that the scheme for a statistical account of Bombay quoted as an appendix to Vol.I. of the late Sir J. M. Campbell's "Bombay Town and Island Materials," while proposing the collection of many details about the roads, makes no allusion to the names of roads. Under the heading of Bridges, however, in that scheme "name and origin of the name" are included among other points of interest to be discovered, and in the more recent Gazetteer of Bombay City and Island, by Mr. S. M. Edwardes, considerable attention has been paid to the general subject of names. But the scope of the Gazetteer did not permit anything like a full investigation of this by way of history, and it is hoped that the following pages may be found of some service both by students of Bombay history and by those august bodies which have to consider the problem of naming and renaming the streets and roads of the City. The author is conscious of the fact that in many cases the explanation here offered of the origin of a name is open to objection on historical or etymological grounds. But books on place-names always contain a good deal of fiction. Canon Taylor, for example, in his entertaining "Words and Places" blindly accept the "good bay" derivation of Bombay which is generally acknowledged to be no more than ingenious fiction. No pretense is made that the following pages are free from fantasy or error, but the compiler will be well satisfied if his critics will join him in the etymological chase. "In all ages," writes Mr. Edward Thomas in the introduction to a recent edition of Canon Taylor's book, "place names have been favorite beasts of the chase. They are a noble game, and they have given the marvelous sport. They continue to do so and generation after generation they survive to fascinate and elude us." In Bombay, the sport is still rather uncommon. When it has more devotees there will be found more consideration in giving names.

For some reason or other, in many places besides Bombay, the importance of names has come to be ignored, they are bestowed and discarded for the most inadequate reasons, and when they survive—either as personal names or place–names their origin is often forgotten. It is convenient and not wholly unjust to blame the Church for this state of affairs.

The first two questions in the Catechism contained in the Book of Common Prayer are: "What is your Name?" and who gave you this Name?" The Catechist, having so far satisfied his curiosity, goes on to ask a number of other questions, but unaccountably omits to inquire "Why did your Godfathers and Godmothers choose that name for you?" The omission may be explicable on the ground that no feminine hand had a share in the compilation of the Catechism a Betsey Trotwood[1] would have put the question in the most searching manner and would probably have expressed her opinion on the suitability of the name with no little ferocity. Even the male authors of the Catechism might have been expected to know better the value and importance of names. Solomon observed that a "good name is rather to be chosen than great riches" and it is indeed to a learned divine, Lawrence Sterne, that mankind is indebted for the *locus classicus* on this subject (Tristram Shandy Chapter XIX). The Shandean philosophy was as follows: "There was a strange kind of magic bias, which good or bad names, as he called them, irresistibly impressed upon our characters and conduct... How many Caesars and Pompeys, he would say, by mere inspiration of the names have been rendered worthy of them? And how many, he would add, are there, who might have done exceeding well in the world, had not their characters and spirits been totally depressed and Nicodemus'd into nothing" It was this passage which inspired R. L. Stevenson with the idea of his essay on The Philosophy of Nomenclature." He adds little of value to what Sterne said, but his conclusion is worth quoting "But, reader," he says, "the day will come, I hope, when a paternal government will stamp out, as seeds of national weakness, all depressing patronymics, and when godfathers and godmothers will soberly and earnestly debate the interest of the nameless one, and not rush blindfold to the christening." In another essay on "The English Admirals," Stevenson wrote: "Most men of high destinies have high sounding names. Pym and Habakkuk may do pretty well, but they must not think to cope with the Cromwells and Isaiahs. And you could not find a better case in point than that of the English Admirals."

But the importance of a good and appropriate name had been recognised in much earlier times. For example, Camden's "Remaines concerning Britaine" (published 1605) has an entertaining little discourse on the subject. Plato, he says, might seeme, not without cause, to advise men to be careful in giving faire and happy names: as the Pythagoreans affirmed the minds, actions, and successes of men to be according to their Fate, Genius, and Name. One also well observeth that these seven things Virtue, good Parentage, Wealth, Dignity, or Office, good Presence, a good Christian name, with a gracious Surname, and seemely attire, do especially grace and adorne a man.... As the common Proverb, Bonum nomen, banum omen."

That proverb has not always been borne in mind in Bombay, as the following pages will show. There has not often been noticeable here the "touch of names," though many legends and not a little history have been handed down from generation to generation in the place-names and street-names of the city. But the majority of names are dull, unimaginative, and reminiscent of dull people of no account. There is little here comparable with the fanciful beauty of many names in Burma.[2]

Few of the street-names and this surely is strange in so commercial a city, are of any commercial value even. It would be absurd to deny that there can be such a value, for all must know the importance of a "good address" to which philosophers and novelists continually allude. For example, in that entertaining novel "The Lost Tribes", by George Birmingham, Mrs. Dann from America discourses on the name Druminawona. "There's money in the name Druminawona, especially when connected in the public mind with a Miracle Play.... We'll boom Druminawona into European celebrity. There's a spaciousness about it which leaves the imagination room to saunter round. There's a kind of meandering melancholy which you'd hardly beat among the best place—names in the itinerary of the children of Israel. Ije-Abarim is a good name, I don't deny it . . . But it's a lap or two behind Druminawona in the race." This aspect of nomenclature is one which all corporators, professors of civics, and omniscient civilians should study with attention.

Perhaps Municipal administrators do not read novels: if they did they would realize there's much in a name. No one knew that better than Dickens. But it is Balzac[3] who has given the fullest analysis of the relation between a man's name and his personality when writing of the sinister significance of the name "Z. Marcas".

"That Z. which went before Marcas, which was seen on the address of his letters, and which he never forgot in his signature, that last letter of the alphabet. Marcas Repeat to yourself that name composed of two syllables, do you not find in it a sinister significance Does it not seem to you that the man who bears it must be a martyr? Although strange and barbarous, that name nevertheless has the right to go down to posterity it is well compounded, easily pronounced, and short as all celebrated names should be. Is it not as soft as it is odd but, further, does it not seem incomplete? I would not take it on myself to affirm that names have no influence on a man's destiny. Between the facts of life and the names of men, there are secret and inexplicable. Concords or visible discords which surprise one; often correlations remote but effective are revealed in them." And Balzac goes on to interpret the hidden meaning of that hieroglyph Z." "Do you not see in the construction of the Z an impeded movement? Does it not represent the random and fantastic zig-zag of a tormented life? What wind has blown on that letter which in every language in which it has found a place commands scarcely fifty words?" "Examine," he again insistently calls upon the reader, "that name Z. Marcas The man's whole life is in the fantastic assembly of these seven letters. Seven! "The most significant of the cabalistic numbers. Marcas, does it not give you the notion of something precious that is broken by a fall, with or without noise?"

It may be said that Balzac exaggerated the significance of a name. But there is, all the same, both with people and places a kind of relation between the name and the personality or place real enough to cause a shock when there is an incongruity between the qualities we had fancied the name to connote and those in the bearer of the name. For instance, a disreputable street bearing an honored name of which there is more than one example in Bombay is a displeasing thing, an argument if ever there was one, in favor of the hateful, American system of numbering streets.[4] In Bombay, there is no system, but many of our roads are named after bygone Governors and makers of Bombay. The result is curious: we associate, for example, Sir Philip Wodehouse with the era of flats and high rents, Sir Bartle Frere with bad road surfaces, Sir George Arthur with desolation. But in few cases is the name appropriate in many the eponym would be ashamed to see the street that bears his name. This is a strange irony. Equally ironical may be the misinterpretation of a name. A famous divine used waggishly to emphasize the word called in the eleventh verse of chapter nine of the Acts.[5] But the street survives, unless the Turks have destroyed it, conspicuous by its straightness in the maze of meandering bazaars in the ancient city of Damascus.

It is curious to note how Bombay has escaped certain typical classes of street names. The system adopted by Latin nations of affixing historical dates to thoroughfares has never had much success with the English, so it is not surprising that Bombay has no equivalent to the Rue de Quatre Septembre of Paris and the Via x x Septembre of Rome. But how comes it that the tendency to name streets after living politicians—other than viceroys and governors—has not spread to India?

We have no Morley Street in Bombay.[6] Nor do wars and battles inspire our Municipality as they do the civic authorities in England, and notably those of Manchester. At present, next to Waterloo and Trafalgar, Alma is the battle most frequently commemorated in England in this way. It occurs nine times in suburban London, but London is outdone by Leeds, which has ten Almas, and Leeds by Manchester, which has fourteen. Inkerman occurs twice in London, twice in Birmingham, and three times in Manchester, which the last city must hold the record for warlike nomenclature. Manchester, in addition to her ten Trafalgars and eleven Waterloos, com memo rates Ladysmith, Khartoum, Sedan, Strasburg, Lucknow, Blenheim, Hastings, and even ancient Troy. Avoiding those types of name, Bombay has derived many of its street-names as one would expect in the East—from castes or occupations. Then it has a fine mixture of English, Parsi, Hindu, and Mahomedan family names, the English being a far larger group than the others and the Portuguese being, somewhat unexpectedly, almost negligible in size. Among other large groups of names are those derived from mythology and places of worship, trees, tanks, and physical peculiarities, while a fair number of names have been imported direct, ready-made so to speak, from other parts of India.

Although the renaming of streets in Bombay has not been carried very far, the subject is one to which attention should be paid. The Mr. Gilders of one generation (see Gilder Street) are liable to be forgotten and supplanted by the Lords Lamington of the next but street names are changed for all sorts of reasons besides that involved in the case just referred to. The war has accounted for a wholesale changing of names on the continent, after the fashion of that from St. Petersburg to Petrograd; but Bombay is fortunate in having no Teutonic names to be eliminated. Gratitude also may sometimes be the ostensible cause as the following two instances will show:-

The Municipality of Kavala has telegraphed to President Poincare begging him to allow the name of France to be given to one of the boulevards of the town in order to recall to future generations the debt of gratitude they owe to France for the inclusion of Kavala in the new Greece. M.Poincare has acceded to the request of the Municipality, and the French Legation at Athens has been instructed to communicate the telegrams exchanged to M.Venezelos. (*The Times*, September 16th, 1913)

The Lisbon Municipality has decided to give the name of London to one of the principal streets of the capital as an expression of gratitude for the reprieve of the man Oliveira Coelho, who was recently sentenced to death, at Liverpool for the murder of his wife on board a British steamer on the high seas. (*The Pall Mall Gazette*, June 9th, 1914)

The latter case is peculiar because Coelho had no connection with England until he was taken to Liverpool and tried. The Portuguese Government urged that he should not be executed on the ground, amongst others, that there was no capital punishment in his own country. The defence was set up that he was not of sound mind, but an appeal failed. The circumstances, to an English mind, hardly seem to call for commemoration by such an act as that proposed by the Lisbon Municipality.

In London, convenience and not sentiment has made necessary a great deal of renaming. The following account of it is given in the L.C.C. List of the Streets and Places (1912 edition). At the beginning of 1857, the Metropolitan Board of Works commenced the arduous task of simplifying the nomenclature and numbering of the streets of London by working steadily through a long list of renamings and renumberings suggested by the Post Office. The first case dealt with was that of the "New Road" which was formed in 1756-7 (under an Act of Parliament) between the "Angel" at Islington and the Edgware Road as a continuation of the City Road to connect Paddington with the City. The number of subsidiary names, as Angel, Terrace, Euston Place, York Buildings, etc., in the thoroughfare was no less than 55. The Board's Resolution was as follows:

"That the portion of the New Road between Edgware Road and Osnaburgh Street be called Marylebone Road; the portion between Osnaburgh Street and King's Cross, be called Euston Road and the portion between King's Cross and the Angel Inn, at Islington, be called Pentonville Road, and that all the separate names of places at present existing in the line of the said New Road, be abolished." The numbers were applied on the odd and even principle, and this system of numbering has been substantially observed in all subsequent renumberings.

In 1889 the London County Council succeeded the Metropolitan Board of Works, and since that date about 1500 streets bearing repeated names have been renamed and 3500 subsidiary names abolished. The success that has been obtained in this direction must be regarded as considerable when it is borne in mind that renamings, particularly in the case of business and more important thoroughfares, are often opposed by the residents affected, who regard themselves as arbitrarily chosen victims of reform, and plead that not theirs but the other streets of the same name should be renamed.

Opposition to the renaming of streets has not been confined to London. There have been occasional instances of it in Bombay, but no one case from Bombay is quite so instructive as the following from Calcutta:-

An interesting little study in street nomenclature is afforded by a petition which has been sent to the Chairman of the Calcutta Corporation by ratepayers and residents in Doorgadass

Mukerjee's Lane, Grey Street. The lane was converted from a *cul de sac* into a public thoroughfare through the efforts of the late Babu Doorgadass Mukerjee, and was named after him. The name has now been changed to Raja Benoy Krishna Lane, but the people of the vicinity strongly object to the alteration, declaring that they "always cherish and revere with the utmost love and esteem the hallowed memory of the late Babu Doorgadass Mukerjee, whose name is almost a household word in the locality," and urging that the lane "ever reminds the people of the locality of the honoured name of a devout and revered Brahmin" to utter which is regarded by the Hindus as an act of piety. Apparently, the reason for changing the name was to avoid confusion with another lane at Kidderpore, but the petitioner argued that the other lane is eight miles off, that they have never had any cause of complaint as to the delivery of their letters, and that their lane should be allowed to retain its old designation, which it has borne for about thirty-five years. As a general rule, it may be admitted that if the name of a street to r lane is associated with any local memory this is an excellent reason for its preservation. (*The Statesman*, January 13th, 1914)

Another case of renaming may be quoted from Calcutta. In that city, churches, temples, and mosques have given their names in whole or in part to a number of streets. So too in Bombay, and in some cases, not a little labour has been required to discover what is the place of worship vaguely hinted at by some such name as "Church Street". The kind of difficulty by which the inquirer may find himself surrounded is well illustrated in the following case. There used to be in Calcutta a "Portuguese Church Street", but the name, according to *The Catholic Herald*, (May 1914), suddenly disappeared. One day the old name board was taken down and yielded its place to "Synagogue Street". Had this been due to the sudden conversion *en masse* of the inhabitants of the street to the Jewish faith, *The Catholic Herald* would surely have had some explanatory comment to offer. But all it said was—"The reason why remains a mystery. We have indeed three synagogues in our neighbourhood, but one is in Pollock Street, the second in Canning Street, and the third in Old China Bazar Lane. Which of the three can boast of having given its name to Portuguese Church Street, which has no synagogue?"

The cases just quoted show the necessity for the observance of some system in renaming streets and Calcutta has done well to take precautions against haphazard changes. In September 1916, *The Statesman*, in announcing that the Calcutta Corporation had appointed a Committee to formulate some kind of policy in regard to the naming and re-naming of streets said: "Some scores of historic names have been obliterated, and a corresponding number of meaningless new names have been introduced. Very often a name is changed simply because some family wishes to have its name given to a street as a cheap way of gaining immortality. Later on, when the family is forgotten, some local worthy earns a reputation for benevolence by giving four annas to a blind beggar, and his relatives and friends demand that the name of the old family shall be expunged and the name of the new benefactor substituted."

This leads one on to another aspect of the question. If residents in a certain street object to its being renamed, they may in rare instances be allowed a voice in the original selection of the name. In such cases what motive would determine their choice? The reader can best answer that conundrum by considering what name he would select for the street he lives in. Possibly his reply would not be free from a suggestion of egoism but here is an interesting example to show that worthier motives may possibly suggest a choice of names. It is taken from the minutes of the Bombay Municipal Corporation for February 1913:

Considered—Letter to the President, dated the 30th December 1912, from the Joint Honorary Secretary, Matunga Residents Association: "We beg to suggest that new foot-bridge erected on the Matunga Station be named after our popular Governor Sir George Clarke, and the new carriage track connecting the

Vincent Road with the bridge be called 'Lady Clarke Road'. We trust this will meet your approval."

Proposed by Mr. Jafler Rahimtoola seconded by Mr. Shapoorjee Sorabjee Mistry: "That the letter, dated the 30th December 1912, from the Joint Honorary Secretary, Matunga Residents Association, suggesting that the new footbridge on the Matunga Station and the new carriage track connecting the Vincent Road, with the bridge, be named after His Excellency the Governor and Lady Sydenham, is recorded."

The most subtle renaming, however, is of an almost accidental kind, when in the process of time the spelling of a name is gradually changed until its origin becomes unrecognisable. Gunbow Street well illustrates this; and the process may actually be seen going on today, for many of the Municipal nameplates give incorrect versions of a name. It is no uncommon thing to find a name rightly spelled at one end of a street and wrongly at the other. Carelessness and ignorance of the kind which turns Medows Street into Meadow Street cause many changes. Others again may be said to be deliberate and attributable to fashion. When the Madras Government in 1688 adopted a proposal to name the streets of Madras one was called St. Thomas Street. Colonel Love, in *Vestiges of Old Madras*, suggests that "had the apostrophe been generally recognised in the manuscript of the period St. Thomas Street would, doubtless, have been written St. Thoma's Street. In the next century, it was often called St. Thome Street, but its present designation is St. Thomas's Street."

A time no doubt will come when the whole problem of naming and renaming streets will be greatly simplified. It will then be a matter of hard cash and the aspirant to immortality will buy the right to affix his name to a street. There should be no difficulty in assessing the amount to be paid, which, on an average, might be about the same as that paid for a C.I.E. The writer does not claim to have originated this pleasing idea on the contrary he has taken it from *The Times* (February 3, 1915) which prints the following:

CICERO AND SANITATION.
THE PRICE OF IMMORTALITY.

We have received from Savona, Italy, the following printed appeal to generous "lovers of classical memories" in quest of immortality. The price of immortality is £2,000. The words "From a village stricken by the earthquake" were added in writing by the sender, apparently as an after-thought and stimulus.

(From the Village Stricken by Earthquake)
To Lovers of Classical Memories

A commune, which derives its name and its origin from the great friend of Cicero, Pomponius Atticus, situated in one of the most smiling valleys of the Apennines, in a fertile and well-tilled region amid hills full of classic memories, seems destined to enjoy a respectable future if it can secure those improvements which progress demands. Hitherto it has been able to secure roads to save it from isolation, schools with suitable buildings, lighting, drinking water, but it has not, and never can, secure the sums necessary for a complete clearance of insanitary areas without which any improvement of hygiene, cleanliness, and aesthetics is impossible.

Whoever should offer the amount fixed by the experts would be entitled (£2,000) to give his name to the main street. In the principal square a monument would be erected to him, and every year he would be commemorated in the church, was he a Catholic, or, in the schools and at the Town Hall was he of another religion.

The Municipality promises this formally, in the hope of finding a generous man worthy to unite his name with the immortal name of Pomponius Atticus.

For further information apply to Guido Cofolla, via' Montenotte, 21, Savona, Italy.

N.B. The amount will be deposited either with the Mayor or with the parish priest, or in a public institute, or with a notary, as may best please the donor.

The chief objection to adopting in India any such scheme as

that just outlined is that the natives of this country have the habit of calling streets, or portions of a street, by unofficial names derived from some obvious characteristics. The reader has only to turn to the explanation of the origin of Abdul Rehman Street, which is given in this book, to find a good example of this custom of dual nomenclature. Bombay cannot claim to be peculiar in this respect for Mr. Hardiman, lecturing at Rangoon in September 1916, showed that the Burmese follow the same custom. *The Rangoon Times* added the comment:

"Any person who tells a gharrywallah to go to Calcutta Road will be taken without delay to Phayre Street. The Calcutta boats used to sail from the foot of what is now Phayre Street, and the name has stuck. Similarly with regard to Mogul Street; too many Rangoon people it is even more familiar as 'Chettys' Road'. There are no less than 106 Chetties in that Street on the voter's list of the Hindu Community and the total must be considerably more, as not all of them take the trouble to have their names entered as voters."

It may be expected that, as time goes on, the picturesque vernacular suffixes[7] will disappear and there will be no more *Mohollas, Wadis,* and *Oarts,* but the deadly monotony of road and street will take their place. Even so, some principle will have to be observed for the two words are not interchangeable. A wholly satisfactory answer to the question "When is a road, not a road?" will never be obtainable, except in new districts where a hard and fast rule can be observed. The question has even been brought into court, and not long ago a resident of North Finchley, London, (see *The Times,* September 26, 1913) objected to his address being given at the Revision Court as a "road" when it was really an "avenue". The distinction is upheld in the London County Council regulations dealing with the naming of streets and the numbering of houses formulated under Part IV of the London Building Act of 1894. The term "road" is there expressly confined to such thoroughfares as may be deemed to be of "sufficient length or importance"; and the

Council's favourable consideration of applications to use the terms "avenue" and "grove" is stated to be conditional upon "the planting and maintenance of suitable trees in the streets in question."

In commenting on that distinction, *The Times* said: "These regulations are valid only within the administrative county of London and apply primarily only to new streets, but there can be no doubt that their existence must exercise some influence in the adjoining suburbs, and that in the course of time a certain measure of uniformity will be achieved over a considerable area. Whether the distinctions drawn by the County Council are to be justified, either on the grounds of etymology or of fact is another matter. Were they suddenly to require naming now, Oxford-street and Regent-street would presumably have as strong claims as Edgware-road and Tottenham-court-road to the enjoyment of the title 'road'. So long, however, as the fundamental principle underlying these distinctions is not flagrantly absurd, it may be accepted without cavil, and the Council is certainly wise in not attempting to imitate the methods of Procrustes and to bring important thoroughfares with names of long-standing within the strict limits of its regulations."

The article in *The Times* just quoted goes on to say: "A firm insistence upon appropriate nomenclature may prove of some value to the cause of social reform. Theoretically, at any rate, there is no greater justification for the landlord who deliberately misnames the thoroughfares on his property than there is for the tradesman who applies a false description to his goods. If the word 'avenue' does, in fact, bring tangible advantages to the owner of the property, it is only fair to insist that he, in turn, should lay out the land in such a manner as to vindicate the appellation." On this suggestion, that there should be any cash difference between a street and a road—any tangible advantage to the owner or to the municipality—an interesting comment is afforded in the following note by a correspondent of *The Manchester Guardian* (March 1914). He states that while in Blackburn recently he discovered a number of streets which had lately, with the consent of the Corporation, been altered from streets to roads. The person responsible for the alteration had a fine and impartial taste in politicians, for "Winston Road" was neighbored by "Beresford Road", but the tenants who now lived in a "road" had to pay for the privilege; their rent was raised sixpence a week from the date the change was made. Most of the tenants seem to have thought that an increase in social dignity derived from the alteration was worth the money, and they paid it willingly. One wonders what the cost of an avenue would have been.

Bombay appears to furnish no examples of disputes as to when a road is an avenue or a street, but Calcutta has been vexed with the similar problem of when is a ditch not a ditch. For instance, the Kalighat People's Association lately passed a resolution: "That in view of the fact that the Hon'ble The Government of Bengal are now prepared to duly consider objections and suggestions in a matter regarding 'Tolly's Nala' (*vide Calcutta Gazette*, dated 11th October 1916), this Association begs most respectfully to object to the name this sacred streamlet is officially called by, as aforesaid in preference to the holy name she goes by throughout Hindoostan among the Hindoos and humbly suggests the restoration of her proper name 'Adi Ganga', being in fact not a despised '*Nala*' (ditch), but a water held in the deepest reverence by the Hindoos, as the Jordan in Christendom."

Finally, it seems essential that a more liberal use of explanatory tablets should be introduced in Bombay. Waudby road, for instance, is one of the few exceptions—as the following pages will show—to the general rule that in Bombay there are no finger posts to history. The tablet system appears to have originated in London where the County Council piously preserves the memory of the departed great by affixing tablets to the houses in which they lived. It would be impossible to put up these interesting little contributions to history in every street that bears the name of some forgotten hero, nor would it be desirable. But in the case of new roads, there should be no difficulty. If we are to have a Kingsway let there be a tablet underneath the name-plate, explaining that the street was so called during the reign of King George V. Even Kings and Queens, with their perplexing dates, are soon forgotten. Few people are much the wiser when they are told that Queen's College, Oxford, is called after Queen Philippa, and Queen's College, Cambridge, after Margaret of Anjou. There was a King's lunette in the old Fort in Bombay, but whether called after a monarch or not it is difficult to say. There is an Alexandra Road in Bombay, one of a little group in Gamdevi which owe their names to the species of tree planted along them by the Improvement Trust: these are Laburnum Road, Alexandra Road, and Cirrus Avenue. To the principle here followed there can be no objection, for place-names derived from trees are common throughout India, but these names are rather severely botanical. Everyone knows a laburnum when he sees one in flower, but the writer will probably not be alone in making the confession that he has no idea what Cirrus or an Alexandra look like. The Queen-mother will, of course, be thought to be the Alexandra referred to, whereas she is presumably godmother to the tree and gives her name only by that indirect method to the road. Scores of similar puzzles will be found in the following pages, and frequent failure to detect the reason for certain names being applied to streets may persuade those concerned in naming our streets that even the greatest of us are ephemeral, liable to be ignored by a posterity which will probably pay as little attention to local history—unless it be forced on their notice—as does the present generation. Yet some consolation may be derived from the fact that Bombay is not peculiar in this respect.[8]

Abdul Rehman Street. *(Crawford Market to Pydhoni.)*
The origin of this name has been traced with much labour by Mr. R. P. Karkaria. At first, he was inclined to think that the street is named after a famous saint or *pir*, Abdul Rehman, whose

shrine on the Cathedral rock, near Kalyan, is known to many in Bombay. The compiler of this book, having discovered that in the early nineteenth century there was in Bombay a well-known horse dealer named Abdul Rehman, thought that worthy might have been the man after whom this noted thoroughfare was called. But Mr. Karkaria discovered that the eponymous worthy was neither saint nor horse dealer, but a Konkani Mahomedan— who flourished 150 years ago—once the owner of most of the land in this locality. After his time Sir Jamsetji Jeejeebhai, 1st Baronet, (1783-1859), came to own large properties here and a section of this street is commonly known to this day as Batlivala *Mohola*, or street, *Batlivala* being the Baronet's surname.

This street has several sections known to Indians by different names: Batlivala Street (as above); *Machhi* Bazaar, fish market, there is one in the locality up till 30 years ago; *Bangribazaar*, the market for bangles, there were shops of bangle dealers; and *Rangari Mohola*, street of dyers.

Adam Street. *(From Apollo Pier⁹ to Lansdowne Road.)*

Named after Mr. J. Adams, executive engineer and teacher of architectural drawing, Sir J. J. School of Art. He designed the Yacht Club Chambers (*see also* Stevens Street). The street is called Adam after a man called Adams on the same principle of perversity which leads many people to speak of an Adams ceiling or mantelpiece when they mean it has been designed by one of the famous brothers Adam.

Adams Street. *(West Agripada, 1911.)*

Near the Adams Wyllie Hospital. (See Wyllie Road.)

Agiary Lane. *(From Borah Bazaar to Mint Road.)*

Named after an Agiary, or Fire Temple, of the Parsis known as Maneckji Seth Agiary, built by Maneckji Nowroji Sett 1748), the owner of Nowroji Hill, in 1733 (*vide* Bombay Bahar, by Wacha, p. 445). Rebuilt 1891. (Parsi Dharmasthal by Patel, p.8, also p.364; and da Cunha, p.297.)

st Agiary Lane. *(From Sheikh Memon Street to Dhunji Street.)*

Named after an Agiary, or Fire Temple, of the Parsis known as Kappawala's Agiary, first consecrated in 1857 by Shapurji Kappawala's (1777-1856) daughter in memory of her father and according to his testament. (Parsi Dharmasthal, p.146.)

2nd Agiary Lane. *(From Sheikh Memon Street to Dhanji Street.)*

Named after an Agiary, or Fire Temple, of the Parsis known as Muncherji Bomanji Seth's Agiary. It was founded in 1796 by his son, Sohrabji Manockji Seth (Parsi Prakash, I.81); and was rebuilt in 1822 by the heirs of Mr. Sohrabji Manockji Seth and again in 1896 by Mr. Framji Hormusji Seth and other trustees. This Muncherji Seth was connected with the Seth family, the owners of Nowroji Hill and builders of the Agiary in the Fort known as Maneckji Seth's Agiary. (*Vide supra* Agiary Lane.)

Agiary Street. *(Bhendy Bazaar.)*

Named after an Agiary, or Fire Temple, of the Parsis known as Mewawala Agiary, which was first consecrated in 1851 by Bomanji Mewawala in memory of his son, Sorabji, who had died in the previous year. 'Mewa' means fruit, and this Parsi had made his money by selling dried fruits. This Agiary was removed in 1914 to Connaught Road, Byculla.

Agripada.

"Such names as Nagpada and Agripada are obviously of Dravidian origin, *pada* or *padu* being the ordinary Kanarese word for a hamlet." (Bombay City Gazetteer, I. 144.) The district, now developed by the Improvement Trust, seems once to have been occupied by Agris or cultivators. There are three sub-divisions or classes of Agris in Bombay, *viz*: Bhat Agris or rice cultivators, (2) Mitha Agris or salt manufacturers and (3) Bhaji-pala Agris or vegetable cultivators. The Gazetteer states that, according to the most widely known Marathi account, the first immigrants to

Bombay in 1294 included seven families of Agris.

The locality is also called after Hiraji Balaji, a former Patel or headman of the Agris.

Ahmedabad Street. *(From Argyle Road to Frere Road.)*

This road, which was constructed by the Bombay Port Trust and handed over to the Municipality in June 1883, is named after the City of Ahmedabad in Gujarat. The streets over a considerable part of the Port Trust property have been named after towns in Western India.

Akalkot Lane No.1. *(A blind lane from Kandewadi Lane.)*

About forty or fifty years ago there lived at Akalkot a holy saint who was believed by some to be a favourite devotee of the god Dattatraya, and by others to be an incarnation of Datta (Trinity) himself. He was famous for his powers of healing the sick and giving to his devotees the objects of their desires. After his death several persons who were his disciples and who had been given by him some *prasad* or mark of favour—such as paduka, or wooden shoes, or betelnuts, or cocoanuts—founded Maths, or shrines, in his honour in different places. One such Math was founded in Kandewadi Cross Lane which from that time has been called Akalkot Lane. (Rao Bahadur P. B. Joshi.)

Albert Road. *(From Chinchpokli Road to Ghorupdeo Road.)*

Named after the Albert Sassoon Mills situated on the Road.

Sir Albert Abdullah David Sassoon, Bart. (1818-1896), son of David Sassoon, State Treasurer of Baghdad; born there and educated in India, his father having first removed to Bushire and then to Bombay, where he established a banking and mercantile house; head of the firm in 1864; made many handsome donations to Bombay, including the Sassoon Wet Dock at Colaba; settled in England; made a Baronet 1890; died 1896.

Alexandra Road. *(Gamdevi. I. T. Scheme IV. Road 4, 1911.)*

Because of the description of the trees—Alexandra laurels—planted by the Improvement Trust along this road.

Ali Umar Street. *(From Banian Road to Erskine Road.)*

Named after Shaikh Ali Umar, a *mistry* or carpenter, who has a house there.

Altamont Road. *(A blind road from Hermitage Pass.)*

Named after a Bungalow called "Altamont". According to Douglas (Glimpses of Bombay, p.47), it let in 1865 for Rs. 1,000 a month. The steepness of the road and the height of the hill suggest that the origin of the name is to be found in mere geographical peculiarities—"high hill road". It would be more romantic if one could trace some connexion with that Colonel Altamont "with very black hair and whiskers, dyed evidently with the purple of Tyre", who was in the service of the "Nawab of Lucknow" and who appears—a sad rascal—in the pages of Pendennis.

Ambroli. *(Girgaum.)*

"It was on the 29th March 1832 that the germ of what became the General Assembly's Institution was established as the Ambrolie English School, connected with the Scottish Mission." (*Life of John Wilson*, by Dr. G. Smith, p. 78.)

Rao Bahadur P. B. Joshi writes: "I am of opinion that the name is a corruption from the old name of the locality. It appears to be derived from *umbar*, a fig tree *(Ficus Glomerata)* and *ali*, a lane. So the original name appears to have been Umbarali or Umbrali. There are other instances of the name. For example, the village near Sopara in the Bassein taluka of the Thana district is called Umbrali. *Ambra* is Sanskrit for the mango, and native Christians may have changed Umbrali into Ambrali or Ambroli."

Anantwady. *(A blind lane from Cathedral Street.)*

Named after a Hermitage of a holy Hindu saint by the name "Anant-Rishi".

Kalbadevi Road

View of Bombay from Malabar Hill

Annesley Road. *(A blind lane from Lamington Road to B. B. & C.I. Railway.)*

Perhaps named after General Annesley who commanded the Bombay District about 1880.

Anstey Road. *(A blind road from Altamont Road.)*

Named after Mr. T. C. Anstey, who lived there. Thomas Chisholm Anstey (1816-73) was for long a well-known figure at the bar of Bombay. He had a very chequered career having been a professor of law, a Member of Parliament (1847-52), and Attorney- General at Hongkong. Anstey was somewhat eccentric and led the life of a recluse, though in his profession he was very successful. Douglas, who gives an account of Anstey in *Bombay and Western India* (Vol. I., p. 234), says: "*Punch* has immortalized him. He recommended that the annual search for a Gunpowder Plot, in the vaults of the House of Commons, should be abandoned, as T. C. A., M.P., was wet blanket enough for any conflagration."

Antop Hill.

Rao Bahadur P. B. Joshi writes: "The name of this hill, like the names of Babulnath hill, Nowroji's hill, appears to have been given from the name of the Hindu or Portuguese owner or proprietor of the hill. It may be either from Antone or Antoba. The former according to the rules of the phonetic changes of the Prakrit language is not plausible because the final 'n' cannot be changed into p. The name Antop is therefore derived from the name Antoba or Antob, the final 'b' being pronounced as p. The hill was Antob's hill and must have been so called and the name appears to have been corrupted into Antop either by Portuguese or English writers. Antoba or Antob is a popular and common name among the old Hindu residents of Bombay, and a late Assistant Secretary to Bombay Government was called N. Antoba. He was an old Hindu resident and landed proprietor and possessed properties at Girgaum, Varli, etc."

Apollo Bandar.

Apollo Street.[10] *(From Elphinstone Circle to Colaba Causeway.)*

"The origin of Apollo (Bandar) is still undetermined. In Aungier's agreement (1672-74) it appears as Polo, while in 1743 it is written Pallo; and the original form of these words is variously stated to have been Palva (a large war-vessel) and Pallav (a cluster of sprouts or shoots). A fourth derivation is from Padao (small trading-vessel) known to Bombay residents of the seventeenth and eighteenth centuries as the class of vessels chiefly used by the Malabar Pirates. Of the four derivations that from Pallav is perhaps the most plausible." (Bombay City Gazetteer, I. 25.)

Maclean's Guide to Bombay quotes the following derivation by Sir M. Westropp: "Polo, a corruption of Palwa, derived from Pal, which, *inter alia*, means a fighting vessel, by which kind of craft the locality was probably frequented. From Palwa or Palwar, the bunder now called Apollo is supposed to take its name. In the memorial of a grant of land, dated 5th December 1743, by Government to Essa Motra, in exchange for land taken from him as the site for part of the fort walls, the pakhade in question is called Pallo." (*Naorojee Beramji v. Rogers.* High Court Reports. Vol. IV. Part I.)

According to a letter to the Municipality, published in *The Times of India*, 23rd March 1916, part of Apollo Street is known to the residents as "Dust Locality".

Apollo Bandar is inscribed Wellington Pier. (q. v.)

Arab Lane. *(From Grant Road to Bapty Road.)*

Probably named after the Arab Pearl Merchants who live in this Lane. There is another explanation to be found in the story that an Arab ascetic, who pretended to possess supernatural powers, put up in this lane about forty-five years ago, and the lane was called after him. This Arab was befriended by several prominent people, one of whom, being childless, was said to have faith in this man who promised him, children.

Ardesir Dady Street. *(From Girgaum Back Road to Falkland Road.)*

Named after a rich Parsi gentleman Mr. Ardesir Dady Seth (1757-1810), a banker, much respected in his own as well as other communities. Sir Bartle Frere said that Duncan, the Governor of Bombay, caused the Cathedral bell to be tolled as his funeral passed by as a mark of respect from the ruling community. (Frere's Speeches, p. 320.) He also built Dady Seth's Agiary in Hornby Road, Fort, and his father Dady Nasserwanji (1735- 1799) built Dady Seth's Fire Temple in Phanaswadi.

Argyle Road.[11] *(Known as Mandvi-Carnac Bandar.)*

Constructed by the Bombay Port Trust and handed over to the Municipality in two portions, one on 30th June 1883, and the other on 18th July 1891. Named after the eighth Duke of Argyle (1823-1900) who was Secretary of State for India from 1868-74.

Armenian Lane. *(From Tamarind Lane to Esplanade Road.)*

Named after an Armenian Church situated in Medows Street close by, which was erected by the early Armenians at the end of the eighteenth century. The Armenians "resided mostly within the Fort enclosure, where they have left the legacy of their name to the Armenian Lane". (Da Cunha, p. 294.)

Arthur Road.[12] *(Bellasis Bridge to Parel Chawl Road.)*

Arthur Bandar Road. *(From Colaba Road to Cotton Green.)*

Both the above are named after Sir George Arthur, Bart., Governor of Bombay, 1842-46. He was born in 1784 and entered the army in 1804. Served in Italy, Egypt, Sicily, and the Walcheren expedition. He was successively Lieutenant Governor of British Honduras, Lieutenant-Governor of Van Diemen's Land, and Lieutenant-Governor of Upper Canada before coming to Bombay. Baronet 1841, Lieutenant-General and Colonel of the 50th Regiment. Died in 1854.

Arthur Crawford Market. *(West of the junction of Hornby Road and Carnac Road.)*

The first part of it was opened in 1868, and the rest in 1869. "At a meeting held on 26th April 1868, on the motion of Dossabhoy Framji, Esq., seconded by Captain Hancock, Mr. Crawford's name was associated with the Esplanade Market." (Michael, *History of the Municipal Corporation*, p.480.) A marble tablet on the north wall of the building bears the following inscription: "The Arthur Crawford Municipal Market erected 1868 on the initiation of Arthur Travers Crawford, C.M.G., I.C.S., Municipal Commissioner of the City of Bombay, 1865-1871."

Mr. Crawford. (1835-1911) took a leading part in improving Bombay.

Ash Lane. *(Esplanade Road to Medows Street.)*

This and its neighbour Oak Lane are not easy to be explained. Ash may have been a man and Oak, unusual as a name, may have been given as a twin-name. Dean Lane in the vicinity is another subject for guess-work.

Assembly Lane. *(A blind lane from Ardesir Dady Street.)*

Named after a building in the occupation of Christian Missionaries who used to assemble there, called Free General Assembly's Institution. This institution is otherwise known as Dr. Wilson's School from the famous Dr. Wilson (1804-75) who founded it and was for long its principal.

Attar Street. *(East of Parel Road, Bhendi Bazaar.)*

So called from there having been shops of perfume sellers in the locality. The word is the Arabic *itr*, perfume. From this is derived attar, a perfume. Hobson-Jobson quotes the analogous Via Latterini in Palermo and the Atarin in Fez.

Babula Tank Road. *(From Jail Road East to Parel Road.)*

Babula Tank called after the babul or *acacia arabica*. (Campbell, III, 595.) The tree in question is a thorny mimosa common in most parts of India except the Malabar Coast. (See Hobson-

Jobson.) The tank of this name formerly existed by this road, but a great portion of it was filled up in 1907.

This is one of the many tree derivations which are disputed. Mr. Karkaria maintains that the tank is called after a man named Babula who lived in the vicinity. (*See also* Babulnath.)

Babulnath Road. (*From Chaupati to Chaupati Road.*)

Constructed by the P. W. D. for the City Improvement Trust and handed over to the Municipality on the 30th June 1901. Named after the Hindu Temple of Shiva called Babulnath which is on a hill close by. Mr. R. P. Karkaria states that "babul" in this connexion [*sic*] has nothing to do with the *acacia arabica* tree, but the temple is called Babulnath after "Babul" the Hindu carpenter who first consecrated the "ling" of Shiva here. Babulnath is like many other names of deities in Bombay and elsewhere eponymous of its consecrator Babul. This information about the name of the carpenter Babul was confirmed by way of inquiries on the spot from temple people. It is also to be found in K.Raghunathji's *Hindu Temples of Bombay*, No. 89, p. 38.

Rao Bahadur P. B. Joshi states that the temple was named Babulnath because the expenses of the consecration of the ling of Shiva were borne by a Somavanshi Kshatriya named Babalji Hirji Nath. It means God, and therefore the temple deity was called Babul Nath, or the god of Babul, by the Yajurvedi Brahmans who consecrated it.

Bakehouse Lane. (*From Forbes Street to Rampart Row.*)

Named after a Government Bakery that existed here.

Bala Mia's Gullee. (*From Lady Jamsetji Road to Mogal Gully.*)

Balaram Street. (*From the junction of Falkland and Foras Roads to Grant Road.*)

Named after Rao Bahadur Eallappa Balaram (died 1914) whose residence was on this road. He was born in 1850 at Colaba, where his father had come to stay some ten years before. His

grandfather and his father were known to the British army at
Poona, Bombay, Deesa, and Karachi as suppliers of milk on a
large scale. After his father's death Mr. Ellappa tried for some
time to continue his ancestors' business; but, after being initiated
in the work of building contractors by Shet Nagu Sayaji, one of
the well-known contractors in the Telugu Community, he found
that the business of milk supplying was not so lucrative. He,
therefore, concentrated his whole energy on contractor's work
and in the Bhandarwada reservoir work and fortification works
at Colaba and Mahaluxmi his capacity came into evidence and he
succeeded in establishing his reputation as a first-class building
contractor. (*Times of India,* September 1914.)

Ballard Pier and Road.[13] *(From Mint Road and Frere
Road Junction to a new road along seashore eastwards.)*
Called after General J. A. Ballard, R.B., who was the first Chairman
of the Bombay Port Trust, holding the post from June 1873
to May 1876. General John Alex Ballard (1830-80) was in the
old Bombay engineers. He saw service in the Crimean War and
was at the siege of Sebastopol. He was also under Omar Pasha
commanding a Turkish Brigade. He also served in the Indian
Mutiny. He became Mint Master, Bombay, in 1861, and when
the Port Trust was constituted in 1873, became its President. He
died on 2nd April 1880 near the battlefield of Thermopylae. He
was the son of a Calcutta merchant (cf. Buckland Diet. Indian
Biog., p. 24). Also a longer notice by Sir A. J. Arbuthnot in Diet.
Nat. Biog. (2nd edition), Vol. I., pp. 1005-6. Kinglake refers to
Ballard's gallantry (Crimean War, Vol. I). There is a brass floor
slab to his memory in the centre aisle of St. Thomas' Cathedral.

The name Ballard is said to be derived from the *ball*, a white
streak, a word of Celtic origin. It was used, according to Wyclif,
by the little boys who unwisely called to an irritable prophet
"stey up ballard" or as the Authorised Version says "Go up thou
bald head." (2 Kings II.23. Quoted in Weekley's *The Romance of
Names.*)

Bamanjee Street. (*From Bora Bazaar Street to Raghunath Dadaji and Gunbow Streets.*)

Formerly known as Nanabhoy Bomanji Street, this very old lane is named after Nanabhoy Bomonji Seth, a noted landlord among Parsis in the latter half of the eighteenth century. He belonged to the well-known Seth family of the Parsis, and Nowroji Hill, Mazagaon, was named after his uncle Nowrosji Rustomji Seth (1662-1732). The dates of Nanabhoy Bomonji are not known, but his signature occurs on various documents from 1748—when he must have been at least 20—to 1799. His younger brother, Muncherji Bomonji Seth, died 8th August, 1799, aged 87.

Banam (or Benham) Hall Lane. (*From Girgaum Road to Girgaum Bach Road.*)

There was originally in this oart, which consisted of cocoanut and plantain trees, a single garden-house named Wan or Ban Mahal, meaning "the house in the wood"—ban or wan (wood) and *mahal* (house). Hence the lane came to be called Ban Mahal Lane. Mr. Acworth, Municipal Commissioner, 1890-95, receiving letters addressed from this lane, while on leave at home where he resided in a house called "Benham" at Malvern, suggested its change of name from "Ban Mahal" house to "Benham Hall Lane" from his Malvern residence and this was adopted. (Facts supplied by Rao Bahadur P. B. Joshi who lives in this lane.)

Banganga Road. (*From Walkeshwar Road round the Tank.*)

Named after the tank bearing this name which is so called because the god Ram feeling thirsty is said to have caused water to spring here by striking an arrow into the ground. Ban, arrow, Ganga, sacred water, (*cf.* for the legend about the Tank and Temple, K. Raghunathji's *Hindu Temples*, M. 26, p.3,4, etc.)

Banian Road. (*From Kika Street to Parel Road.*)

From Bania or Vania, Hindu trading castes that have houses

there. (For the caste of Vanias, vide Bombay Gazetteer, Vol. IX, Part I. Hindus of Gujarat, pp. 69-81, etc.)

Bank Street. *(Elphinstone Circle to Custom House Road.)*
Named after the Bank of Bombay premises situated in this road. "In 1862, when the Elphinstone Circle scheme was brought forward the Bank took up land there and commenced the erection of the present building, which was completed, and to which the Bank was removed in 1866." (*Bombay City Gazetteer*, III p. 220.)

Bapty Road. (*From Grant Road to Parel Road.*)
Named after Mr. James Bapty, the former owner of a flour mill situated at the corner of the road at its junction with Falkland Road. Bapty owned a bakery which was formerly well known in Bombay for its bread and especially pastry. "Bapty's Cakes" were long famous. Pearse succeeded to his business.

Bapu Hajam Street. (*West of Parel Road, Bhendi Bazaar, near Pydhonie.*)
So named after the house of Bapu Hajam, a Konkani Mussulman, who was a prominent member of the Hajam, or barber, trade, and also practiced circumcision among his people.

Hajam (Arabic) a barber: they act as surgeons also, and their women as midwives and nurses. They are Sunnis. (Whitworth's Anglo-Indian Dictionary.)

Bapu Khote Street. (*Kalbadevi Road to Ersakine Road.*)
According to one informant, it is named after a Mahomedan, Bapu Khote, who was a famous barber and a Hakim. Another explanation is that it is named after a Konkani Mahomedan Khote, landowner, called Bapu, to whom this land once belonged. Bapu, originally a Hindu name, has been adopted by Konkani Mahomedans. This street is locally known as Jambuli Mohola, i.e., Jambul colour street, because it is occupied by Mahomedan dyers and this jambul, or violet, colour is conspicuous there among the dyed clothes exposed to dry.

Bhendi Bazaar

Colaba Causeway

Barber Lane. *(From Cawasji Patel Street to Pitha Street.)*

Mr. E. P. Karkaria in *The Bombay Gazette*, 7th October 1907, expressed the view that this lane was so called, because barbers had houses in the locality, just as Gola Lane is called after Golas who resided there.

It was proposed in 1907 to change the name to Barbican Lane, but the proposal was not adopted. In 1915, another change was proposed and the subsequent discussion in the Municipality and the Press was carried on with no small display of acerbity. To begin with, the Municipal Commissioner (Mr. P. B. Cadell, CLE.) wrote: "I have the honour to state that certain persons living near Barber Lane in the Fort, have asked that that name should be altered. Although it is possible that the lane was originally named after a Police Officer, named Barber, and was not so called because of its use by persons working as barbers, the latter origin is by a natural process generally associated with the name. The lane itself has been greatly widened and improved by Municipal action, and although it is not generally desirable to change a name simply because some people are dissatisfied with it, yet in this case, as the highly respectable people who live in the houses abutting on the lane wish for a name more in consistence with its improved condition, I think that their wish may be gratified. I have the honour to propose therefore with the sanction of the Corporation that it be called 'Bakhtawar' Street. The word in Persian and Gujerati means fortunate and may be taken to convey the good fortune of the street in having such respectable people living near it and in having been brought so prominently to the notice of the Corporation." Mr. V. A. Dabholkar suggested the lane might be named Sukhia Street— after Dr. Sukhia, a member of the Corporation. Sir Jamsetji Jejeebhoy advocated changing "Barber" into "Barbour"; and Sir Dinshah Wacha, who deprecated changing historical names, said members had humorously suggested different names; but he did not know if the Corporation would relish his humour, if he suggested that the street be called "Bhadbhad Street", in consideration of the fact that so many loquacious persons lived there. No alteration was as a fact made.

From among many letters which subsequently appeared in *The Times of India*, two may be selected. Mr. R. D. Cooper wrote from 12th Lane, Khetwadi, that Barber Lane was really known as Hajam Mohola, being a rendezvous of barbers (Arabic, *hajam*). "I think," he said, "the 'Policeman Barber' is a mythical personage invented for the purpose of the debate. The probability is that it derives its source from 'Barbary' as some of the Barbary pirates had their dens in the street. They were rich with their ill-gotten gains and some of them must have purchased some properties." Mr. H. Sibbald (aged 70) writing from Santa Cruz, turned the policeman into a doctor. He wrote: "I joined the Customs in 1864. In those days it was an eyesore to see a steamer in the harbour. Once a month the P. & 0. Boats came with mails, otherwise, 200 to 300 sailing ships were in the harbour. In those days there were two doctors for the shipping named Bolt and Reynolds, the former lived in the lane and the latter at Colaba. About 66 Bolt left for England, and Barber took his house and place, Reynolds also went about that time, and Dr. McGregor took his place. In those days doctors engaged to a ship got Rs.100—a tidy sum—and filled their pockets soon and left. I think the street name must have been given about that time by the Municipality, I am not certain, but this much I know that respectable people lived in that quarter and Dr. Barber was one of them." Mr. Karkaria remarks upon this theory: "This doctor of 1866 could not possibly have given his name to the lane, for the name Barber Lane is at least a generation older. I have come across it in the files of *The Bombay Gazette* for 1839."

Bardan Street. *(From DeSouza Street to Kazi Sayad Street.)*

Named after the Gujarati word Bardan, meaning gunny bags, which are sold on this road. Formerly it was called Essaji Hamji Street (*cf.* Note on Samuel Road).

Baroda Street. *(From Carnac Siding Road to Frere Road.)*

Named after the city of Baroda.

Barrack Street. *(From Bazaar Gate Street to Mint Road.)*
Named after military Barracks situated there. They were formerly known as the King's Barracks (the king being George III), because the Royal Troops, as distinguished from the East India Company's, occupied them. Even now elderly Indians call this King Burakh Gully, King Barrack Lane.

Barrow Road. *(From Colaba Causeway to Merewether Road.)*

This road was constructed by the Bombay Port Trust and handed over to the Municipality in 1897. It is named after Mr. H. W. Barrow, for some time head reporter of *The Times of India*, and subsequently from 1870 to 1898, Municipal Secretary.

Bastion Road.[14] *(From Murzban Road to Theatre Road: constructed by the City Improvement Trust, and handed over to the Municipality on 18th August 1904.)*

Several roads in the locality are named after the old fortifications, e.g., Ravelin Street. There were 8 Bastions, called respectively: Prince's, Royal, Old Mandvi, Marlborough, Stanhope, Church, Moors, and Banian. (*Bombay Gazetteer*, Materials Vol. 26, part 2, p.286, etc.).

Battery Street. *(From Apollo Pier to Lansdowne Road.)*
Named after the Saluting Battery which was situated on this road until it was transferred to Middle Ground.

Bawankhani Lane. *(A blind lane from Chaupati Road.)*
There may be an allusion to the residence of women of bad repute: *bhairon* in Marathi meaning women, usually prostitutes, devoted to service in a temple. Bavankhandi literally means large chawl of bavan, fifty-two, khans or rooms. There is a similar and well-known place of the same name in Poona City, after which this lane is most probably called.

Bazaar Gate Street.[15] *(From Bori Bunder to Elphinstone Circle.)*

Named after one of the three Fort gates. It was situated at the north end of the street, leading into the old Fort. This Gate had two smaller gates also, hence it was known to the natives as Teen Durwaza, or Three Gates. The gate was pulled down in 1862.

Bazaar Gullee. *(From Mahim Bazaar Road to Mahim Bazaar Cross Road.)*

Named because of a general market close by.

Beach Road. *(From Colaba Road westward.)*

It runs close to the foreshore.

Beef Lane. *(From Parsi Bazaar Street Westward.)*

Sir Dinshah Wacha writes: "It was so called because the beef was sold here for the town barracks soldiery. I am not sure whether the kine were also slaughtered here. This lane is just opposite the Military Stores Lane, adjoining Graham's office to the north. At the east end of Military Stores Lane, you will notice the back part of the married men's barracks, and a little beyond are the old Town Barracks and it is to be presumed that the military folk kept all military requirements near each other within easy distance. So the other military stores were all stored in that lane. The beef had to be supplied apart and could not be allowed to be in the same place as the other stores. The old Commissariat was also in Parsi Bazaar Street."

Bell Lane. *(From Esplanade Road to Medows Street.)*

So named after Messrs. Bell & Co., who had offices there.

Bellasis Road.[16] *(From Parel Road to Bellasis Bridge inclusive.)*

An inscription on the Bridge reads as follows: "A.D. 1863. This Bellasis Road was made in 1793 A.D. by the poor driven from the City of Surat in that year of famine, out of funds raised by public subscription, and takes its name from Major-General

Bellasis under whose order it was constructed."

"Bellasis Road, the great drive towards Scandal-point at Breach Candy, is in the recollection of many now living a small straggling, uneven, jolting pathway, got up by General Bellasis of the Artillery, to suit his convenience, as he lived in the proximity of the famed Maha-Laxmi; and from thence he was to be seen jogging in his native *ghari* drawn by a couple of oxen." (*The Monthly Miscellany of Western India*, May 1850.) There is a mural monument to Major-General John Bellasis and his wife in St. Thomas's Cathedral. On it, he is described as commanding officer of the forces and Colonel of the Regiment of Artillery on the Bombay establishment. Died, February 11, 1808, aged 64. General orders by Government, Bombay Castle, 16th Feb.1808: "It is with sincere concern that Government announce to the Army the death of that very respectable officer, Major General John Bellasis, late Commanding Officer of the Forces, who departed this life, on Thursday, the 11th instant, suddenly, whilst he was in the meritorious discharge of his duties, presiding at the Military Board, thereby terminating a long course of zealous and faithful services." According to Mr. E. Weekley (*The Romance of Names*, p. 142), Bellasis is a Norman name from *bel assis*— fairly situated. But the same writer in *Surnames* (p. 318) says there is a font-name Belle Assez which is not uncommon in Middle English and would give the same result. A friend informs me that the motto of the family is *Bel Assez*, fair enough, and this is certainly a more complimentary derivation than *bel assis* which might be interpreted "well seated".

Belvedere Road. *(From Dockyard Road to Wari Bunder Road.)*

This must be called after a once famous bungalow on Bhandarwada hill. It was from that house that Sterne's Eliza (Mrs. Draper) eloped with a naval officer.

Bhai Jiwanji's Lane. *(A blind lane from Girgaum Road.)*

Named after the owner of the oart, Mr. Bhai Jiwanji, who was

Managing Clerk of Messrs. Crawford, Solicitors. He was a great book collector and had a valuable library which was dispersed after his death in 1906. He was well-to-do and possessed several properties in Bombay.

Bhajipala Street. *(From Abdul Rehman Street to Memonwada Road.)*

Bhajipala, or vegetables, are sold here.

Bhandari Street. *(From Falkland Road to Bhandarwada Street.)*

This street, as well as Bhandarwada, is called after the Bhandaris, or toddy-drawers, that resided there. Some of them possessed houses and were reckoned among the old residents. Others came to Bombay from Malvan, Vingurla, and other places, and settled in the seventeenth and eighteenth centuries.

"The Bhandaris whose name is derived by some from the Sanskrit *mandharak* (a distiller) and by others from *bhandar* (a treasury) constitute one of the oldest communities in Bombay Island and are sub-divided into five classes—Sinde, Gaud, More, Kirpal, and Kitte or Kitre—which neither dine together nor intermarry." (*Bombay City Gazetteer*, I. 231.)

Bhandup Street. (From Musjid Siding Road to Coorla Street; Constructed by the Bombay Port Trust, and handed over to the Municipality on 30th June 1883.)

Named after the village of Bhandup situated on the G. I. P. Railway in the Thana District.

Bhangwadi or 2nd Kolbhat. *(A blind lane from Kalbadevi Road).*

"In this oart," says Rao Bahadur P. B. Joshi, "there were formerly afforded good facilities for persons who were accustomed to drinking Bhang. Several shops were opened by Gujarati Brahmans for the preparation and sale of this drink. Various kinds of Bhang were prepared, such as Bhang mixed with milk and sugar, and Bhang mixed with pounded almonds, cardamoms, saffron, and other spices. The prices ranged from half an anna to two annas per tola, or a bowlful. On Hindu holidays and fast days such as the Mahashivaratra, Mondays of the month of Shravan, etc., there was a great demand for this Bhang by the devotees of Shiva. It is believed to be sacred to Shiva and therefore people partook of it on days sacred to that god. It was also poured by way of *Abhishek* (holy sprinkling) on the ling of Shiva."

Bhang is the dried leaves and small stalks of hemp *(i.e., Cannabis indica).* The word is usually derived from Sanskrit, *bhanga*, breaking, but Sir Richard Burton derives both it and the Arab *Banj* from the old Coptic *Nibanj* "meaning a preparation of hemp; and there it is easy to recognise the Homeric Nepenthe." *(Hobson-Jobson.)*

Bhasker Lane. *(A blind lane from Cathedral Street.)*

Named after the father of Mr. Anandrao Bhasker, who was a Judge of the Small Cause Court, and who owned a large property here. Bhaskerji was a Prabhu by caste, and most of the houses around this locality and Bhuleshwar were owned by the Parbhus and the Yajurvedi Joshis till the middle of the nineteenth century.

Bhaskar Bhau Lane. *(Near Gamdevi.)*

This lane is called after Bhasker Bhau Mantri who possessed several houses in Gamdevi and other parts of Bombay. He belonged to the Somavanshi Pathare Community and was a well-known contractor in Bombay.

Bhattia Bagh.[17] *(South of Victoria Terminus.)*

Sir Dinshah E. Wacha, otherwise "Sandy Seventy" in *The Bombay Chronicle* (April 9, 1915) says: "It was not till 1861, generally after 1864, that Malabar Hill began to be well populated. The remaining population in the Fort, especially the north, was occupied by Parsi merchants and traders, the Kapole Banias, men of the rank and wealth of Mangaldas Nathoobhoy and Vurjivandas Madhowdas lived here and there in central townhouses which still stand. Next were the wealthy Bhattias, who resided in Bazaar Gate Street and in Old Mody Street, lying parallel to the east, in the direction of Mody Bay. Goculdas Tejpal, Goculdas Liladhar Pasta, Khatao Makanji, Jivraj Baloo, Jairam Sewji and such occupied the Bazar Gate Street from the north end as far as the Parsi Agiary Street, south. In Holee Chukla also the population was Bhattia. This extended as far as Parsi Bazaar Street, near the end of Gola Lane. Generically it was known as 'Bhattia Wad'. The 'Bhattia Bag' in Fort Street, now under renovation, was so called, because all along its south side the Bhattia population greatly preponderated when the 'bag' so-called was first built in the latter part of the sixties."

When the Municipality undertook to lay out the Bagh, which had grown untidy and unsightly, in an orderly fashion various suggestions were made for its re-naming and in May 1917, it received the official designation Victoria Square. "The name," said *The Times of India*, "is obvious enough when one remembers that the Victoria Terminus is one of the boundaries of the area thus rechristened, but 'square' is geometrically indefensible. 'Place', which was originally suggested, would have done well if only we could acquire the habit of using it in the French sense which somehow does not fit in with the English pronunciation of the word. The Corporation cannot, in any case, be accused of coming to a decision without due consideration of the various names suggested. They have deliberately swept away the name of a quarter which is smaller in size than in historic interest, and, as our Calcutta correspondent pointed out in a letter which we published yesterday, it often happens that the name of a quarter or district is not attached to any street and is thus in danger of being obliterated. For many reasons that are to be regretted."

Bhatwadi. *(From Girgaum Road to Girgaum Back Road.)*

There were formerly three Bhatwadis in Bombay. One of these has been now acquired by the City Improvement Trust (in 1911), and a new street is opened there. These three Bhatwadis at one time formed one oart which was the property of one Bhat Vasudev Sankhedkar, a priest of the Somavanshi Pathares. It contained cocoanut, plantain, and guava trees. It was subsequently divided into three parts after it had passed into different hands. Till the year 1884, the 2nd Bhatwadi was known as Ganesh Ramji's Wadi owing to the fact that most of the houses there were owned by Ganesh Ramji, head surveyor to the Collector of Bombay.

Bhantaz Gully. *(From Portuguese Church, Chiniwadi.)*

Bhavnagar Street. *(Behind Memonwada Street.)*
So-called because the inhabitants are Memons from Bhavnagar in Kathiawar. The Memons in Bombay mostly come from Cutch, Halar, Dholka in Ahmedabad Collectorate, Bhavnagar, Bhuj and Verawal in Kathiawad, and are accordingly called Cutchi, Halai, Dholka, etc., Memons. *(cf.* Bhujvari Street).

Bhendy Bazaar. *(See under Parel Road.)*

Bhimpara Street. *(In Mandvi Koliwada.)*
Named after a Koli called Bhim, who was formerly headman of the Kolis there. The name Bhim originally belonged to a god of the Hindu Pantheon, who corresponds to the classical Hercules. In the guise of Bhim Baja, Bhimdev, or Raja Bimb it appears as the name of the chief who ruled over Mahim in Bombay and Salsette subsequent to the epoch of Silahara rule. *(vide* Bombay City Gazetteer.)

Bhisti Street. *(East of Bhendi Bazaar.)*
So called because Bhisti Mussulmans are the chief inhabitants. Bhistis are water carriers. The word is commonly derived from the Persian *bihishti,* a person of *bihisht* or paradise, but the compilers of Hobson-Jobson fail to trace its history. Dr. Jivanji Jamsetji Modi questions that derivation and thinks it comes from the Gujarati word for "to wet".

Bhoget Gully. *(From Gopi Tank Gully No. 2 to Sorab Mill Gully.)*

Owes its name to the fact that a well-known Bhagat or Deval rashi (exorcist) once resided in its vicinity.

1st Bhoiwada Lane. *(From Kiha Street to Bhuleshwar Street.)*

Named after *Bhois* (palanquin bearers) who inhabited the place. "Boy, a palanquin-bearer. From the name of the caste, *Tel.* and Mal. *boyi.* Tarn, *bovi*." (*Hobson-Jobson.*)

The whole land of the First, Second and Third Bhoiwada is Fazandari tenure. The original Fazandars of all these three Bhoiwadas were Balambhat Javle and other descendants of Gamba Naik Javle, and that Naik who were granted by Governors Sir John Childe (1687 A.D.) and Richard Bourchier (1755 A.D.) patents of rights as the chief hereditary priests and physicians of Bombay. At present the Fazandars of the first and of the half of the 2nd Bhoiwada are the descendants of the said Gamba Naik and Vithal Naik Javle. The Fazandari rights of half of the 2nd Bhoiwada, including the Bhuleshwar Market, and of the whole of the 3rd Bhoiwada are vested in Mr. Vinayakrao Sadanand Joshi, the present owner of Sadanand Joshi's oart and properties in Bombay.

Bhujvari Street. *(Memonwada.)*

The inhabitants are Memons from Bhuj in Cutch. (*cf.* Bhavnagar Street.)

Bhuleshwar Street. *(From Kalbadevi Road to Girgaum.)*

"So called from the great temple and tank of Bhuleshwar." (*Bombay City Gazetteer.*)

"Bholesvar is one of the epithets of Siva, Bhola meaning 'simple' hence he is called the Lord of the Simple. Others say that it was built by a rich Koli by name Bhola, who, having neither progeny nor relatives of his own, spent his large fortune in the building of this temple, which bears his name. Another tradition connects the temple with a Pardesi by name Bholanath, who built it whence the god is called by his name. Others say that the Pardesi was a mere porter of the temple." (Da Cunha, p. 61.) Rao Bahadur P.B. Joshi writes: "The statement that Bholeshwar is one of the epithets of Shiva is not accurate, because grammatically it would be wrong to form the compound Bholeshwar from Bhola and Ishwar. Such a compound would be considered a hybrid combination. The real origin of the name Bhuleshwar is from the name of the individual who built the temple and gave money for the consecration ceremony. Originally the temple was built by a local Koli, or fisherman, who was wealthy but had no progeny. His name was Bhula or Bhulya, and so the God was called Bhuleshwar by the officiating priests who were the hereditary Yajurvedic Brahmans of Bombay. In Bombay, several other temples are similarly named after the person who built them."

Bibijan Street. *(From Abdul Rehman Street to Chakli Street.)*
Named after Bibi Jan (Bibi, lady, in Hindustani), a noted resident of the locality in the last generation.

Bohra Bazaar Street. *(From Fort Street to Gunbow Street.)*
Shops on this road belong mostly to Bohras, hence the name. "The Bohras are the descendants of Hindu converts to Islam and claim connection with the missionaries sent forth by the Fatimite Khalifa of Egypt in the fourth and fifth centuries of the Muhammadan era; they are excellent businessmen and are engaged in every branch of trade and commerce from retail dealing and tin-working to broking, contracting, and the exploitation of industries." (*Bombay City Gazetteer* II, p. 180)

Bohra Musjid Street. *(From Bohra Bazaar Street to Jijibhai Dadabhai Lane.)*
There are eight Bohra mosques in Bombay, of which one is in this street.

Bombay.

The name is so exhaustively examined in the *Bombay City Gazetteer* (Vol. I, pp. 19-24) that no more than a summary of the various derivations need be given here.

DeCastro, writing in 1538, said the island was called Boa Vida (Good Life) on account of its groves, game, and abundance of food.

Fryer wrote (1673) of the "convincing denomination Bombaim quasi Boon Bay." Grose (1750) refers to "Buon-Bahia now commonly Bombaim." These are commonly recognised as mere attempts to explain the more ancient Musalman and Hindu names, Manbai, Mambai, or Mumbai, which were turned into Bombain (occurs in 1508): Mombaym, Bombain, Bombayim (Portuguese, 16th century) : Bombaye and Bombaum (1666), Bombeye (1676), and Bombay or Bambai, which occurs in 1538 and finally came into use in the 18th century.

Another fanciful derivation is from *mubarak* (lucky) because the island was the first land sighted by seamen voyaging from Arabia and the Persian Gulf to Sopara, Chaul, and Thana.

"Prolonged investigation leaves little room for doubt that the word Bombay is directly derived from the goddess Mumba, the patron deity of the pre-Christian Kolis, the earliest inhabitants of the island; and it only remains to ascertain the original form of the goddess's name." (*Gazetteer*, Vol. I., p. 21.)

Rao Bahadur P. B. Joshi, in his short sketch of the *Early History of Bombay*, writes: "By some authorities, it is firmly believed that the word is derived from Munga or Muga, the name of the Koli who first built the temple of the goddess Mumbadevi. But, we generally find that whenever any Hindu deities are called after the name of the builder of the temple, the name of the male builder is given to the god and that of the female builder, or of the male builder's wife, is given to the goddess. The feminine of the word Munga is Mungi, and therefore, the correct form would have been Mungi-ai and not Munga-ai or Mumba-ai. Another explanation of the origin of the word Mumba is, that it is derived from Amba, another name of Bhawani, the consort of Shiva (the Hindu god of destruction); and in our opinion this latter explanation is correct. As the goddess Kali is sometimes called Mahakali or the great Kali, so Amba is also called Maha Amba or the great Amba, and by the Kolis and other illiterate persons, the word Maha-Amba is generally pronounced as Mamba or Mumba. The suffix *Ai* signifying mother is a term of respect applied to Hindu goddesses. The word Mumbai is, therefore, derived from

the words Maha+Amba+Ai= Mumbai; and evidently, the word Bombay (Portuguese *Bombaim*) is the corruption of the word Mumbai." *See also Bombay Town and Island Materials.* (Vol. Ill, pp. 644-647.)

Borebhat Lane. (*From Girgaum Road to Cow Lane.*)

Named after the garden of *Bor* trees *(zizyphus jujuba)* that existed here. (*Bombay City Gazetteer*, p. 26.) The Bor tree is well known, because of its fruit, which is oval and pulpy, about the size of a plum. The dried fruit is the jujube of Arabian and Persian books on materia medica and is used in Europe in the preparation of syrups and lozenges.

Bori Bunder

Mr. R. P. Karkaria writes: Bori or more commonly Bora or Borah, is the name of a well-known Mahomedan sect in Gujarat whose followers are numerous in Bombay. But what particular connection these people have with the Bunder cannot be ascertained. Perhaps the name might be derived from the 'bor' tree, and these 'bor' trees might have grown on the original site of the Bunder.

"Bori Bunder was constructed in 1852 before which date it was a small landing place for boats greatly obstructed by rocks and shoals, which were in that year blasted and a capacious Bunder with large accommodation for passengers and goods erected. When the G. I. P. Railway was being constructed, all the rails and machinery from England were landed at the Bunder which is in the vicinity of its terminus and the Railway station, first built in 1853, was called Bori Bunder Station until 1887 when it was replaced by the present large and handsome building, and got its name of Victoria Terminus from the fact that it was opened in the year of the Jubilee of Queen Victoria."

Brae Hill.

It may be the Scotch word "brae", but is more likely an English corruption of *Ambrai,* meaning the mango-grove. (*Bombay City Gazetteer*, Vol. I, p. 14.)

Breach Candy. *(See Hornby Vellard.)*

Bread Market Street. *(From Mint Road to Modi Street.)*

It formerly led from the Fort Market to the Bread Market, the site of which is now occupied by the Wadia Fountain.

British Hotel Lane. (*Blind lane touching Apollo Street.***)**

Named after a hotel of the same name. Douglas ("*Glimpses of Old Bombay*", p. 70) reproduces the following curiously spelled advertisement of 1845:

"British Hotel, Bombay."

"For the accommodation of Families and Gentlemen. These spacious premises are desirably situated in the Fort, and within five minutes walk of the Banks of Dock Yard, Custom House and principal House of Agency.

Wines and liquors of the best description. Tiffins and dinners sent out on short notice. T. Blackwell, Proprietor."

Broach Street. (*From Frere Road to Musjid Street: constructed by the Bombay Port Trust, and handed, over to the Municipality on 30th June 1883.***)**

Named after the Town of Broach in Gujarat.

Bruce Lane.[18] *(From Tamarind Lane to Apollo Street.)*

Buran Tank Road. (*From Vincent Road to Naigaum Road.***)**

Mumbadevi Temple

Bombay Port, 1890

Burrows Lane. *(From Girgaum Road to Christian Burial Ground.)*

Named after the Rev. Arnold Burrows, who was in charge of the cemetery at the west end of the Lane. He was Chaplain; 1760-1813. The cemetery was known after him as Padre Burrows' godown. (*Adventures of Qui Hi*, and *Bombay Gazetteer*, Vol. 26, part 2, p. 292, note).

Butcher Island.

In 1701, the Deputy Governor wrote of "Robin the Butcher's Island" on which Campbell (*Materials*, Vol. I., pp. 438-9) has the following note:

"The only apparent sense is that the butcher after whom the island was supposed to be called was named Robin. Perhaps a fairy Robin Goodfellow name suitable to the mythical name giver. In spite of Grose's (1750) explanation (*Voyages*, Vol. I., p.58) that the island was called Butcher, because cattle were kept on it for the use of Bombay, the English name Butcher Island seems a case of meaning-making. Fryer (1673. Travels 61-62 and map) calls the Isand Putachoes (properly Patecas) or watermelons, and this derivation is accepted in a Portuguese account of Bombay, 1728. Patachos, Yachts, a word used by Baldaeus, 1680, and Putas, harlots, in connection with a story that as in Goa a Bishop banished the harlots to an island, have also been suggested. But Patecas, melons, seems the only derivation for which authority can be quoted. Besides the commoner Dardivi, the Marathi name Bhat or Bhatiche Bet; the low lying island, is said to be still in use for Butcher's Island. It seems fairly certain the English Butcher is the Portuguese Pateca. The absence of any connection between the island and watermelons suggests that in its turn the Portuguese name is also a meaning-making from the Marathi Bhatiche Bet."

Byculla.

Campbell (Bombay Town and Island Materials, III. 595) derives the word from Bhayakhala, the *Cassia fistula* (i.e. Indian Laburnum) level, *bhaya* being a local Kunbi form of bawa. Brandis (Indian Trees, p. 253) gives *bahawa* as the Marathi for this tree.

Mr. Karkaria suggests that Bhayakhala may mean "low ground" *bhaya*, ground and *khala*, low. But this is disputed on account of the long a in khala.

Rao Bahadur P. B. Joshi, on the other hand, asserts that Bhaya-khala means the khala or threshing ground of Bhaya (the name of an individual), or the threshing ground containing prominently a bhaya, or bhawa, tree.

Byculla Station Road. *(From Ripon Road to Byculla Railway Station.)*

Constructed by the Improvement Trust as a means of access from Agripada to the station.

Byculla Tank Pacady. *(A blind lane from Agripada lane.)*

This Lane led to Sankli Tank *(q.v.)* which formerly existed to the south of the Khatao Mills, hence the name.

Byramji Hall Lane. *(From Babula Tank Road to Motlabai Hospital.)*

Named after the house called Byramji Hall, the property of the late Mr. Byramji Jijibhoy (1824-1890). The house was at one time the residence of Sir James Mackintosh (1765-1832) Recorder of Bombay, and known as "Tarala". Later the Sadar Adalat was housed in it. (*See* Nanabhoy Byramji Oart.)

Cadell Road.[19] *(See Mahim Bazar Road.)*

Carnac Bunder. Carnac Road.[20] *(Known as Esplanade Cross Road: From Frere Road to Esplanade Road including Carnac Bridge.)*

Named after Sir James Rivett Carnac, Bart., Governor of Bombay, 1839-41. "We learn that Sir James Carnac, on the requisition of Luximon Hurrechunderjee, Esq., has consented to attend the Bunder now in the course of construction by that enterprising gentleman in order to confer upon it the appellation of the Carnac Bunder." *(Bombay Times,* April 28, 1841.)

Carnegy Road.[21] *(Touching Queen's Road to Marine Lines Street.)*

Named after Lieutenant-General A.Carnegy, Provincial Commander-in-Chief, 1887, during the absence on furlough of the Duke of Connaught.

Carpenter Lane. *(From 2nd Carpenter Street to Dockyard Road.)*

Sutar Gully, or Carpenter Lane, so called because in this locality almost all the houses at one time belonged to the *Somavanshi Kshatri*, many of whom carried on the profession of *Sutars* or carpenters. Even to this day, many houses in these lanes are owned by these people. At one time the Somavanshi Pathares and the Pathare Prabhus formed one community.

Sutar is the Hindi form of Sanskrit *sutradhara*—a carpenter so called from the thread (sutar) with which he marks out his work.

Carroll Road. *(From DeLisle Road to Elphinstone Road Station.)*

Named after Mr. E. B. Carroll, Loco. Superintendent, B.B. & C.I. Railway, who retired in 1897.

Carwar Street. *(From Mint Road eastwards to a new road along the Seashore: constructed in 1888.)*

Named after Karwar, the chief town of the North Kanara district.

Cathedral Street. *(From Bhuleshwar Street to Dady Shet Agiary Street.)*

The Rev. Father Hull writes: "This Street is so called because of the Cathedral of Nossa Senhora d'Egperanca. This church was originally situated just outside the Bazaar-gate of the fort on the site of Bori Bunder station being built by the Franciscans before 1600 (perhaps 1596). In 1760 it was demolished by order of Government, and rebuilt on the Maidan somewhere near the old cross still standing at the back of Marine Lines, which seems to have been the church cross in front of the west door. The transfer was due to a decree for clearing the Esplanade for 300 yards round the fort walls for military purposes. (The Mambadevie temple was similarly removed from a spot quite close by Esperanca church and was rebuilt at Pydhoni where it still stands.) In 1804 Government extended this clear space to 1,000 yards round the fort. The 1,000 yards line is still preserved by the line of houses from Queen's Road by the hospital, and through that slum by the Scottish graveyard, and along Carnac Road as far as Crawford Market and on to Carnac Bridge. As Esperanca Church was within this line, it was pulled down again in 1804 and rebuilt in Bhuleshwar where it now stands. But the work was so scamped that it fell into ruin very soon, and in 1832 it was rebuilt again in its present form. It was the chief church of the Vicariate, and became the Cathedral when the Vicariate became an Archbishopric in 1887."

Cavel Street. *(From Dadyshet Agiary Street to Kalbadevi Road and from Kalbadevi Road to Girgaum Road.)*

Cavel was formerly occupied almost exclusively by the aboriginal tribe of the Kolis, who were converted by the Portuguese. Cavel seems to be a Portuguese rendering of Kolwar, a Koli hamlet. (Da Cunha, p.7). Another explanation said to have been suggested by the late Mr. A. M. T. Jackson is that Cavel is a corruption of the Portuguese word for the chapel. The Goanese to this day most associate Cavel with the Church known as Cavel Church, about which the Rev. Father Hull writes: "Its title is *Nossa Senhora de Saude*. It was built as a private family chapel some time about 1794 or earlier and fell under the jurisdiction of the Padroado clergy, who have always retained it. Sonapur chapel, along with Marine Lines, was originally the graveyard attached to Cavel Chapel above described. There was a small mortuary chapel attached; but in about 1905, a new chapel was built covering the whole of the ground. The twin church of Our Lady of Happy Voyage and of St. Francis Xavier in Burrows Lane was built by the Padroado community, 1870-1872."

The native name for the locality is Gaewadi, from *gae*, cow, possibly because beef used to be sold there in shops of which one or two survive, or because cows were kept there.

Chakla Street.[22] *(From Carnac Road to Masjid Bunder Road [23].)*

Abbreviated form of Khalasi Chakla, by which the street was formerly known: *Khalasi* meaning Laskar and *Challa* meaning Rendezvous.

Chamarbag Lane. *(From Government Gate Road to Suparibag Road.)*

Named after a Toddy Oart called *"Chamarbag"*—the shoemakers' garden.

Chambhar Lane. *(From Parel Road to the Foot Bridge over the G. I. P. Railway South of Byculla Station.)*

Considering that the Municipal list of roads (1912 edition) gives the *varia lectio* of Chamber, it is possible that Chambhar has been evolved by carelessness from Chamar, a cobbler.

Champawadi. *(From Sheik Memon Street to Vithalwady.)*

Named after a Champa tree, of which the dead stump is still preserved in the verandah of a house in this gully. This variety of tree is known to botanists as *Michelia Champaca*, a large evergreen tree with yellow or orange flowers, strongly scented. Hindu women use garlands of these flowers as an Ornament in their hair. For a similar derivation, *cf.* Ovalwadi.

Chana Street. *(From Modi Street to Bera Bazaar Street.)*

Named after the shops of chana, parched gram, etc., on this road. *Chana* is Hindi, from the Sanskrit *Chanaka*, the pulse *(Cicer arietinum)* chick-pea, or Bengal gram.

Sir D. E. Wacha under the pseudonym of "Sandy Seventy" in *The Bombay Chronicle* (April 9, 1915), referring to Bombay in the early sixties, says: "A few rich Arabs, Moguls, and Bohras lived in old Mody Street, somewhere from the locality where an old

Musjid stands at the corner of Chana Street. The Arabs had a 'Kava Khana' there. They were mostly horse-dealers, but of a highly respectable and wealthy class. It was on this account that Chana Street is more commonly known as Kava Khana lane." The street is also called chanawallani gulli, i.e., the lane of the grain-sellers.

Chandanwadi. *(From Lohar Street to Girgaum Road.)*
Named after the shops for selling sandalwood called in Marathi, Chandan. "Sandal" is the Arabic form of the Sanskrit *Chandana*.

Charni Road.[24] *(From Queen's Road to Grant Road.)*
A portion of this road was called for a short time Ollivant Road after Sir B. C. K. Ollivant (b. 1846), Municipal Commissioner, 1881-90, and Member of Council, 1897-1902. This road was not formerly connected with Grant Road, but in 1883-84 it was extended to meet the latter road "by making a new road between Girgaon and Khetwadi and partly by widening the street known as Khetwadi 15th Lane" (Michael, History of Bombay Municipality, p. 409). This new extension was in 1884, called Ollivant Road, but the new name merged into the old one of Charni Road as practically it was but one road.

The name Charni or Chendni was brought to this locality, according to Rao Bahadur P. B. Joshi, from Thana. The locality near Thana Railway Station is called Chendni and many inhabitants of Chendni in Thana came and permanently settled at Girgaum, in Bombay, and so-called the locality where they settled Chendni.

Another theory derives Charni from *charon*, the grazing of cattle.

Chaupatti Road. *(From Babulnaih Road, Dadysett Road and Babulnaih 1st Cross Lane to French Road.)*
"Chowpatty is really Chau-pati (four channels) and is evidence of the inroad of the tide before the western foreshore was reclaimed" (Bombay City Gazetteer, I. 27). This name is

analogous to that of Satpaty, a village in the Mahim Taluka of the Thana District, which is approached through a channel or khadi, containing seven pats or divisions of water.

Chewoolwadi. *(Kolbhat, a blind lane from Kolbhat Street.)*

The original residents of this place came from a village, called Cheool, in the Alibag Taluka of the Kolaba District, better known as Chaul (Revadanda). The locality at one time contained several houses of Somavanshi Pathares and Agris of Cheool and of their hereditary priests, the Yajurved Brahmans.

Chikalwadi Lane. *(From Tardeo Road to Sleater Road.)*

Chikkal, mud (Marathi). And rightly so called. During heavy rainfall Chikalwadi is under water, the stormwater drainage being defective.

Chimaji Ramji Street. *(From Nowland Street to Nawab Tank Road.)*

Chimna Butcher Street. *(From Grant Road to 1st Duncan Road Cross Lane.)*

Named after a leading butcher of the same name.

Chinch Bunder Road. *(From Dongri Road to Mazagaon Road and Jail Road East; from Mazagaon and Babula Tank Road Junction to Keshavji Naik's Fountain.)*

Chinch, Tamarind (Marathi).

Chinchpokli Cross Lane. *(From Chinchpokli Road to Ghorupdeo Road.)*

Chinchpokli, Tamarind Dell. Mrs. Elwood in her "Narrative" (published in 1830) spells it Chintz Poglie.

Chini Gully. *(From New Purbhadevi Road to Old Purbhadevi Road.)*

Chira Bazaar. *(Section of Girgaum Road, between*

Thakordwar and Dhobitalao.)

So named because the place was paved with flat slabs of stone or flagstones called *Chira*.

Chor Gully. *(From Suparibag Road to Government Gate Road.)*

Named so because it was a haunt of thieves in former times, Chor meaning "thief" in vernacular.

Chunam Kiln Lane. *(From Grant Road to Girgaum Back Road.)*

Named after the Chunam Bhatti or Lime Kiln that existed here in former times. There was only one kiln. The road was also known as Mangaldas Wadi Road, as on both sides of it there were, and still are, properties of the late Sir Mangaldas Nathubhai (1832-1890) the first Hindu Knight. (*See also* Lamington Road.) There are also a Chunam Kiln Street, Cross Street, and road in the Memonwada locality.

Church Street. *(From DeLima Street to Muzawarpakhada Road.)*

The Rev. Father- Hull writes: "Church Street, Mazagon, off DeLima Street, runs east. It used to run to what was known as Gloria Church, which was pulled down by the Port Trust in 1913 to make room for the Harbour extensions. The Harbour Railway has cut the street off; but beyond the line, it continues to the old cross still standing, which was exactly in front of the west door of Gloria Church. Space, where the church stood, is still unoccupied, and its general outline up to the plinth can be traced still. The original chapel of Nossa Senhora da Gracia was built shortly after the acquisition of the Mazagon estates by a private Portuguese family in 1548 or so. The land subsequently became the property of the De Souza family. The chapel was rebuilt in 1803 and enlarged in 1810. It was served by the Franciscans from its first erection till these, being Portuguese, were expelled by the English in 1720; and the Carmelites of Surat took their place. In 1794 the Bombay churches were divided between the Goa clergy and the Carmelites, and Gloria Church fell to a lot of Goa and was retained by them (Padroado jurisdiction) ever since, till its demolition in 1913. A new Gloria Church was built on Parel Road opposite Byculla station to take its place. It forms a conspicuous object with its massive gothic tower."

Churchgate Street.[25] *(From Elphinstone Circle to Churchgate Station.)*

Named after one of the three gates leading into the old fort. It was situated at the Junction of Hornby Road and Churchgate Street near the site of the present Flora Fountain (today is known as Hutatma Chowk). About 1840, the old gate was rebuilt only to be pulled down twenty years later when the Fort walls were demolished.

"The maintenance of the Fort of Bombay is not only useless but has become a downright and most serious nuisance to the inhabitants at large. It is the source of a ridiculous waste of money to Government itself: witness the erection, not yet completed, of a gate at the cost of Rs.30, 000 to block up the way to the church. The Fort is a costly and fitting nuisance." (A correspondent of *The Times* in 1841.)

"About half a mile from the Apollo Gate, the Church Gate is passed. This is sometimes called the Powun-Chukkee Gate from the circumstances of a windmill (powun, wind—chukkee, mill) having stood there some sixty years ago (i.e. in the late 18th century). There is no published account of it, but from the drawings of the late General Waddington, it appears to have been in the form of those generally in use in the south of England and north of France." (*Buist's Guide*, p. 265.) Dr. Jivanji Jamsetji Modi confirms this and says that in his youth to go to the povanchaki meant to go out of the gate for an airing.

Cirrus Avenue. *(From Gilder Street to Souter Street.)*

After the description of trees planted by the Improvement Trust along this road. It was opened in 1911.

....

54

Clare Road. *(From Bellasis Road to Parel Road.)*

Named after the second Earl of Clare (born 1792, died 1851), Governor of Bombay, 1831-1835. The road was constructed in 1867. (Michael: *History of Municipality*, p. 408.)

Clerk Road.[26] *(From Parel Road to Mahalakshmi and Hornby Vellard Junction.)*

Named after Sir George Russell Clerk, Governor of Bombay, in 1847-48 and again 1860-1862. Sir G. R, Clerk (1800-89) was a distinguished Bengal Civilian, who took a prominent part as a Political Officer in the Punjab and N. W. Frontier. He was Under Secretary of State for India when he came in 1860 to Bombay as Governor. He was a Member of the Council of India, 1863-76. Died 1889.

This road was constructed in 1868. (Michael, *History of Municipality*, p. 408.)

Cleveland Road. *(From Worlee Road to Worlee New Sluice along the west of Channel.)*

Named after Mr. Henry Cleveland, a solicitor and partner in Messrs. Hearn and Cleveland, Government Solicitors. He was one of the few Englishmen who invested capital in land in Bombay. He did not sell his property when he retired but left it to be managed by his Parsi assistant. There is also a Cleveland Bunder called after him.

Clive Road. *(From Musjid Bridge to Elphinstone Bridge.)*

Named after Lord Clive (1725-1774), Governor of Bengal, 1758-60 and again 1765-1767.

Club Road. *(From Lamington Road to Morland Road.)*

It skirts the northern side of the Byculla Club compound. Colaba

"It is a reasonable supposition that Colaba is the same word as Kolaba, the name of the district which lies on the far side of the harbour. One derivation of the name is, from Kolvan or

Kolbhat, a koli hamlet or holding—a view which gains weight from the fact that the Kolis undoubtedly settled here, as in other parts of the island, in prehistoric times, and also from the fact that there was an oart known as Kolbhat on the Island during the early days of British Rule. On the other hand, Molesworth states that the name of the mainland district is a corruption of the Arabic *Kalabeh*, meaning a neck of land jutting

into the sea, a description which exactly fits Colaba." (*Bombay City Gazetteer*, I. 25.)

Dr. Jivanji Jamsetji Modi writes: "I remember having heard when young that Colaba meant the *ab* (Persian for water) of the Kolis, *i.e.*, the quarters of the Kolis fishing in the adjoining waters." Mr. Karkaria points out that Seely in his *Wonders of Ellora*, (1824), derives Colaba from the Persian

cala, black and *ab* water.

Colaba Causeway. *(From Arthur Bunder to Apollo Bunder Road.)*

The Island of Colaba was, in 1838, linked with Bombay, by this Causeway, which had been projected in 1820 but not started until 1835. It was widened and rebuilt, 1861-63. Buist (*Guide* p. 266) gives a different set of dates and a different name to the Causeway. "The Vellard, a raised roadway which connects the two islands of upper and lower Colaba, with that of Bombay. In 1828, the construction of the present means of crossing was commenced—it was completed in 1834 and received the name of the Governor of the day, Sir Robert Grant. In 1852 it was greatly widened and improved."

1st Coly Lane. *(From Nowrojee Street to Gun Carriage Street.)*

So named from the Kolis or fishermen residing here.

Connaught Road. *(From Parel Road to Reay Road.)*

Named after the Duke of Connaught (born 1851), the third son of Queen Victoria. He was Commander-in-Chief, Bombay, from December 1886 to March 1890. Several roads in the neighbourhood have been given names from Ireland, e.g. Cork Street and Ulster Road.

Connon Road. *(From Hornby Road to Esplanade Road.)*
Named after Mr. John Connon (died 1874), Chief Presidency Magistrate, Bombay. He was for long a prominent citizen and Chairman of the Bench of Justices when they managed Municipal affairs before the Act of 1872. For several years, from 1859 onwards, he directed *The Bombay Gazette*. He also took an interest in education among the Anglo-Indian Community and a school was called after him the John Connon High School.

Convent Street. *(From Wodehouse Road to Colaba Causeway.)*
Named after the Fort Convent School. The Holy Name Church, with the Archbishop's house on one side and the school on the other, form- a symmetrical group in Wodehouse Road "which was completed in 1904-05, superseding the establishment of the Fort Chapel.

That Chapel was built by the Carmelites sometime after 1720. Attached was the residence of the Vicar Apostolic, and, after 1886, of Archbishops Porter and Dalhoff. After 1760 when the Esperanca Church was removed to the Esplanade, the Fort Chapel became the centre of the Fort parish. The buildings were renovated in 1846. In 1904 the Archbishop transferred his residence to Wodehouse Road, and the Church of the Holy Name, next door to his house, superseded the Fort Chapel, which in 1905 was dismantled and turned into shops and tenements, as is seen now. Attached to the establishment was the Fort Convent School founded in 1855 by the congregation of Jesus and Mary. This also was transferred to a new building in Wodehouse Road in 1904.

The Rev. Father Hull, Editor of *The Examiner*, who has kindly supplied the foregoing facts, adds *The Examiner* Press in Medows Street, still, part of the old Fort Chapel group, was founded in

1867. A new road has been planned which will cut through the Fort Chapel property and cause the old buildings to disappear.

Coombharwada Cross Lane. *(From Chakla Street to De Souza Street.)*

The place was formerly occupied by Coombhars, dealing inputs, tiles, bricks, etc.

Kumbar (Kanarese) or Kumbhar (Marathi from the Sanskrit *kumbhakara*) a water-jar maker. The name of a caste; they are potters, and sometimes makers of tiles and bricks, and earthen idols also. In Kanara some are dyers. They rank high among Sudra castes. (Whitworth. *Anglo-Indian Dictionary*).

1st Cooper Street. *(From Pakmodia Street to Parel Road.)*

Formerly known as Edulji Cooper Street. Cooper is a Parsi surname. "Cooper is one of the commonest occupative names, a derivative of Latin cupa or cuppa, a vessel." (*The Romance of Names* by E. Weekley.)

Cooperage Road. *(From Wodehouse Road to Mayo Road.)*

The Cooperage, described in 1759, as "a shed the coopers work in", was actually situated within the Dockyard until 1742, when the pressure of space obliged Government to remove it to a warehouse on the water's edge belonging to Mr.Broughton. From that date, the Cooperage continued to occupy hired buildings until 1781, when Rear-Admiral Sir Edward Hughes protested against the proximity of the buildings to the Garrison, and Government resolved to "erect a proper shed upon the Apollo ground for the reception of the King's provisions." This shed has given the Cooperage area its name and was in use until 1886 when the new stores were built in the Dockyard. (*Bombay City Gazetteer*, III, 272).

Coorla Street. *(From Clive Road to Frere Road.)*

Named after the village of Coorla on the G. I. P. Railway in Thana District.

Coppersmith Lane. *(From Moombadevi Road to Abdul Rehman Street) and Coppersmith Street (Dockyard Road to Reay Road.)*

There are coppersmiths' shops in both streets.

Cork Road. *(A blind road from Sussex Road.)*

Named after County Cork, Ireland. (*See* Connaught Road.)

Cotton Green Road. *(From Colaba Causeway to Merewether Road.)*

"The present Cotton Green is situated at Colaba, and was first set apart for the purpose about the year 1844." (*Bombay City Gazetteer*, III, 252). The original Cotton Green of Bombay (the side of which is now partly occupied by Elphinstone Circle q.v.) was called the Bombay Green. This use of the word Green—of which there is a survival in Green Street—can never have been very apt in dusty Bombay. Golfers with rare veracity use the word Brown, and the Cotton Brown on the analogy of 'putting brown', would be a better description. To this fact, attention was drawn in 1839 when were published the anonymous (by Major David Price) *Memoirs of the Early Life and Service of a Field Officer of the Indian Army*. Referring to his residence in Bombay in 1789, the author says:

"Having landed our detachment of the ninth battalion and paraded them under the old tamarind tree on Bombay Green (so-called I suppose like *lucus a non lucendo*, because it seldom or never exhibits that color so refreshing to the eye), we finally conducted them to their barracks on the Esplanade. I then sought my staid and excellent friend, William Morris, and with him, agreed to renew, as long as circumstances would admit, that confraternal plan of living together which had hitherto for so many years contributed so largely to our mutual comfort. For this purpose, we rented a well-built house, about halfway between the Church and Bazaar Gate, at the termination of the back lane opening upon the ramparts which from the occupation of our opposite neighbours we call Shoe-Maker Lane."

Council Road. *(From Hornby Road to Cruickshank Road behind the Municipal Offices.)*

Named either after the Council Hall of the Bombay Municipal Corporation, or, as seems more probable, after the Town Council as the Municipal body was for long known.

Cow Lane. *(From Kandewadi Lane to Mugbhat.)*

"Cows were assembled here every morning before being taken to pasture." The old inhabitant responsible for that statement does not, however, say when the name was given or when the practice was discontinued.

Cowasji Patel Tank Road. *(From Kika Street, Erskine and Falkland Roads to Girgaum Back Road).*

"Owes its name to the son of one Rustom Dorabji who, in 1692, placed himself at the head of a body of Kolis and assisted the English to repeal an invasion by the Sidis. For this good work he was appointed by the Company Patel of Bombay, and a Sanad was issued conferring the title upon him and his heirs in perpetuity." (*Bombay City Gazetteer*, I, 40). This Rustom Dorab is known among Parsis as Rustom General or General. He died at the age of 96 in 1763. The tank was built by his son Cowasji Patel about 1780. He was the first Parsi to settle and have property in Salsette, when it came in 1774 into British hands, the East India Company giving him several villages there. He died in 1799 aged 57. (*The Parsi Patels of Bombay*, p. 20, etc. Also *Bombay Bahar* by R. Vacha, p. 255, etc.). The tank has now been filled in. At a meeting of the Corporation in April 1915, it was stated that Bai Dinbai Byramji Patel had laid claim to the site and had expressed her wish to erect a statue of the donor on the site. The Commissioner stated: "It has always been a public tank and Bai Dinbai has no claim to any ownership. There does not seem any necessity for placing a statue of the original constructor of the tank on the site, as funds would probably not be forthcoming for it but if, as suggested above, the plot is laid out as a garden, it may be called the Cowasji Patel Garden, and a descriptive tablet may be put up in it. This will be quite sufficient to preserve the constructor's name."

Cross Island.

Campbell's *Materials* etc., Vol. III., p.655, has the following: "Also known as Gibbet Island, it is a small rounded knoll about 80 feet above high-water level and 500 yards east of Carnac Bandar. According to one account, this island received its name, because on it the first Portuguese (A.D.1507-1509) set across in a sign of possession. In support of this derivation the common name of the island, Signalo is quoted as proving that on it the cross was planted as a sign or signal. But in Urdu-Marathi *Shinala* means not a signal but a harlot, and this may be the origin of the common Bombay story that certain harlots who were implicated in a murder were the first offenders who were hanged on the cross or gibbet on Cross Island. Of the practice of hanging pirates and other heinous offenders in chains on Cross Island, the author of *Qui Hi* (1816, page 202) has left the following:

> The sails are set, they catch the wind,
> The Elephanta's left behind,
> Dismal the wretched fellows rung
> That on Cross Island's gibbets hung;
> Dismal the kites, and crows, and cranes,
> Shrieked to the music of the chains."

(A footnote in *Qui Hi* says that Cross Island was "a well known Golgotha, near Bombay.")

Cruickshank Road.[27] *(Dhobi Talao to Victoria Terminus.)*

Named after Col. J. D. Cruickshank, of the Bombay Engineers, who retired in 1895. He served some time in Gujarat, and in Aden where he superintended the building of fortifications. One of his sons, in the B. G. A., is now (1917) in the United States supervising, as a British agent, the manufacture of munitions for the Allies.

This road was formerly known to the Indian public as "Vachla Rusta", or "Middle Road" because it was between Hornby and Esplanade Roads.

Cuffe Parade Road. *(From Panday Road to Wodehouse Road in the area reclaimed from the sea by the Improvement Trust).*

Named after Mr. T. W. Cuffe, of King, King & Co., Chairman of the Standing Committee of the Corporation 1901-2. As a member of the Improvement Trust, he suggested the raised footpath which distinguishes this road. He was Commandant of the Bombay Light Horse.

The Municipal Road Book gives the title Cuffe Parade Road, but in general use, the Road is dropped.

Cumballa Hill.

Kambala Hill apparently the grove of Kambal or Kamal also called *shimti*, Odina wodier. (Campbell, III, 595.)

This explanation has an air of deep learning but is rather difficult to support by quotation. Odina wodier is a large tree common in deciduous forests throughout India and Burma. In *Indian Trees* by Sir Dietrich Brandis (published in 1906) a number of vernacular names for the tree are given, but the only one which even remotely resembles that given by Campbell is Kamlai, and that is not a Bombay word, but from the Punjab.

Rao Bahadur P. B. Joshi writes: "In my opinion, the correct name of the hill is *Khambala* and not *Cumballa*. Among the old residents, the hill is known as Khambala tekdi or hill. The hill is close to the Gowalia Tank where the Gowalas or cowherds of Bombay brought the cattle of the locality for drinking water. The hill was a jungle and as in course of time a number of *khambs* came to be fixed there, the place was called *Khambalaya* or Khambala that is an abode or locality of *khambs*. Now, what were these *khambs*? Anyone well acquainted with the folklore and religious observances of the old lower class Bombay Hindu would tell you that these *khambs* were abodes or resting places for the temple ghosts of certain dead ancestors. Suppose in a home or family the lady of the house, or her daughter-in-law, or son, or daughter, has fallen sick, or children die after birth, or any other calamity occurs. What would the old villager do? He generally would send for the *Bhagat* or exorcist. This Bhagat would pretend to be possessed with the spirit of the dead ancestor and would tell the householder that in order to cure the patient it was necessary to pacify the spirit by giving it a fixed resting place. For this purpose a post of the *khair* tree is chosen, nails are driven therein, the exorcist's black thread called nada dora is tied around it, garlands of marigold, *makhmal* flowers are fastened to it, some mantras are recited over it, and then waving it thrice before the face of the patient at evening time it is taken to a selected lonely place and there it is fixed in the ground. The patient or his relative worships this *khamb* periodically that is on the date on which the ancestors died and during the 'Manes Fortnight' which falls in *Bhadrapada*, September."

Currey Road. *(From Suparibag Road to DeLisle Road.)*

Named after C. Currey, Agent of the B. B. and C. I. Railway, 1865-75. In 1876 he was appointed Secretary to the Company in London and held that post until his death in September 1878.

Custom House Road. *(From Elphinstone Circle to Apollo Street.)*

Named after the Government Custom House situated on this road.

Dadar Road. *(From Swparibag Road to the junction of Portuguese Church Street and Lady Jamsetji Road.)*

From the village of Dadar through which it runs. Dadar in Marathi means a staircase or ladder, and as this locality could be regarded as part of a ladder leading to Bombay it was called Dadar. There is more than one instance of localities lying on the outskirt of a village being formerly named Dadar by Koli residents. Thus, for instance, the locality on the outskirt of the village Kelva in Thana District, which is wholly occupied by Koli fishermen, is called Dadar.

Dady Street, or Dady Agiary Street. *(East of Girgaum Back Road, Khetwady.)*

So named after Ardeshir Dady (1757-1810) who formerly owned the large oart through which the street was made. Ardeshir was a rich and respected Parsi Merchant of the Dady or Dadysett family. His father Dady Nasarwanji (1735-1799) was a well-known banker. (*See also* Homji Street).

Dadyshet Agiary Street. *(From Girgaum Road to Kalbadevi Road.)*

The Agiary after which this street is called is really an Atesh Bahram, i.e., Fire Temple of the highest class, there being only three others in Bombay; whereas there are nearly 50 Agiarys or temples of a lower class. This Fire Temple was consecrated in 1783 at the expense of Dady Nasarwanji (1735-99), a rich Parsi Banker, by Mulla Kawoos, the father of the celebrated Mulla Firuz.

Dadyshet Road. *(From Chaupati and Walkeshwar Junction to Babulnath Road.)*

Named after the founder of the Parsi Dadyshet family who left a large property in this neighborhood in trust for the maintenance of the Dady Fire Temple between Guzer Road and Kalbadevi Road. This founder, Dady Nasarwanjj (1735-99), was a broker and banker and amassed great wealth. The Chaupati property was acquired about 1783 from a Portuguese named Barretto. (*Bombay Bahar*, by Wacha, 311.)

Dady Suntook Lane. *(A blind lane in the Dhobi Talao Section of Girgaum Road.)*

Named after Dady or Dadabhai Suntook (born in 1745) who was a noted Parsi horse-dealer, and had his stables here. He had extensive dealings with Arab merchants who supplied his stables. He died in 1824. His son Sorabji Suntook (1800-1862) carried on his business. Both father and son were well known among English sportsmen in Bombay. Suntook is originally a Hindu name.

Dalal Street. *(From Hummum Street to Apollo Street.)*

Dalals (sharebrokers) assemble for business in this street. This street speculation became very prominent in 1913 when the acting Police Commissioner (Mr. R. Mactier) endeavored to interfere with the Dalals in the enjoyment of what they had come to regard as a right, namely, the occupation of this street.

Dammer Lane. *(From Gamdevi Road to French Road.)*

Dammer (a corruption of the Hindi *damar*) means rezin, pitch.

Dariasthan Street. *(From Musjid Bunder Road to Samuel Street.)*

Named after the Hindu Temple called Dariasthan (God of the Sea) which exists here.

D'Lima Street. *(From Dockyard and Reay Roads to Frere Road and Wadi Bunder Road.)*

Named after Lawrence D'Lima, a Portuguese Merchant owning property in this locality.

Dean Lane. *(From Hummum Street to Tamarind Lane.)*

See Ash Lane.

De Lisle Road.[28] *(From Haines Road to New Parbhadevi Road and Elphinstone Road.)*

This road was constructed in 1868. (Michael, *History of Municipality*, p. 408). Named after Lieutenant A. De Lisle, who was appointed Secretary of the Foras Commission in 1851 by the Bombay Government. But after a short time, his place on the Commission was taken by F. Hutchinson by whom the Foras Report was written.

Crawford Market

Flora Fountain

Deodar Bowdi Lane. *(Mazagon.)*

The particular well *(bowdi)* which gave its name to the lane is shaded by a deodar tree.

Depot Lane. *(From Girgaum Road to New Queen's Road.)*

It led to a night-soil depot situated at the end of the lane and was known among the residents of the locality by the name Hagri Galli or Night Soil Lane. The Lane has been absorbed into Lamington Road.

De Souza Street. *(From Masjid Bunder Road to Samuel Street.)*

Dhabu Street. *(From Erskine Road to Grant Road.)*

Formerly known as Baba Dhabu Street. So called from Baba Saheb Dhabbu, a Konkani Mahomedan, who had property there in former days. *Dhabbu* means originally a thick copper piece worth two pice, and is generally used as a nickname for a showy simpleton, in Gujarati.

Dhanji Street. *(From Moomba Devi Road to Mirza Street.)*

Named after a Parsi Dhanji Jamshed Doongaria who lived in this street. He died sometime before 1827.

There was until recently another Dhanji Street, abutting on Girgaum Back Road, called after a Parsi, Dhanjibhai Framji, but that name has been altered by the Municipal Corporation to Procter Street *(q.v.)*

Dharamsi Street. *(From Dhaboo Street to Parel Road.)*

Formerly known as Peerbhoy Dharamsi Street.

Dharavi Road. *(From Siort Road to B. B. & C. I. Railway Level Crossing near Mahim Station.)*

Named after the village of Dharavi near Sion, Bombay.

Dhobi Street. (*From Musjid Bunder Road to Bhajipala Street.*)

On account of the residences of Dhobis (washermen).

Dhobi Talao.[29] (*South end of Girgaum Road.*)

This tank has given its name to a busy locality as well as a lane. But the tank has now been filled in and for some years before that operation took place, the dhobis had transferred their activities to the well on the north corner of the Esplanade maidans. A tablet still (1917) remains in a fragment of the wall that end closed the tank and bears the following inscription:

"Framji Cowasjee Tank. This tank was so called by order of Government to commemorate the late Framji Cowasjee's liberality in expending a large sum of money on its reconstruction in the year 1839."

Dhobiwada Road. (*From Haines Road to Mahalaxmi Station.*)

Named after a Dhobiwada (a public washing place of the city) which is situated along this road. This Dhobis' place was until forty years ago on the site of the present Victoria Terminus, on the erection of which it was removed to Mahalaxmi.

Dhun Mill Gully. (*From Khed Tank to Dhun Mill.*)

Named after a Cotton Mill of the same name, which was founded by the late Nasarwanji Ardeshir Hormusji Wadia, who called it after his mother Dhunbai.

Dhuswadi (Dhobi Talao). (*From Lohar Street to Wellington Street.*)

Dockyard Road. (*From Mazagon Road to Mazagon Pier.*)

The P. & O. The dockyard is situated here.

Doctor Street. (*From Erskine Road to Grant Road.*)

Formerly known as Shaikh Abdul Doctor Street, after a Mahomedan physician, Dr. Khoja Abdulla, of Ratnagiri, who died about 15 years ago and was a noted resident in this quarter. The street is also known as Dhanwady: *dhan* means rice. A section of it is locally known as Tiwali Moholla or street, a name, which it got from a prominent resident, Kutbuddin Tiwali, who was a Konkani Mahomedan and Serang, or foreman, in the Gun Carriage Factory at Colaba.

Dolker Street. *(From De Lima Street to Church Street.)*

Dongarsi Road. *(From Walkeshwar Road to Harkness Road.)*
Probably called after a Bhattia landowner named Dongarsi or Doongarsi.

Dongri Street. *(From Carnac Bridge to Jail Road South.)*
"Dongri, which appears in English writings of the seventeenth century as Dungrey and Dungaree mean the hilly tracts, from the Marathi word Dongar." (*Bombay City Gazetteer* I, 27.) The name will survive the hill, for this dongri, or hill, was long considered by military authorities as a menace to the Fort of Bombay in the hands of an enemy, and they several times recommended it to be taken down and leveled: this has at last been partly done by the City Improvement Trust, though not of course for the old reason. (Campbell, II, pp. 357-361.)

Dontad Street. *(From Musjid Bunder Road to First Chinch Bunder Road.)*
Named on account of two *Tad* trees that existed in this road. *Don* two (Marathi) and *Tad* Palm tree.

Doongri Street. *(East of Parel Road, Bhendi Bazaar behind Pala Street.)*
So named from onions having been stored there formerly, *doongri* meaning, in Cutchi dialect, onions. This Doongri is to be carefully distinguished from Dongri hill *(q.v.)*.

Dubash Lane. *(From Sandhurst Road to Girgaum Back Road.)*
Dubash is the surname of the Parsi, the late Dadabhai Hormusji

Dubash (1832-1896) who had property there. The word dubash has had various meanings (for which see *Hobson-Jobson*) all obsolete in Bombay now except that of a man attached to a mercantile house as broker transacting business with Indians.

Dubra Street. *(North-East of Pydhonie.)*

So named from *dubra*s being stored there. A *Dubra* is a large bottle-shaped vessel made of hides in which ghee or clarified butter is preserved.

Dukar Wady. *(A blind lane from Girgaum Road to Burial Ground.)*

"Duker" means "pig", there having formerly been a small pork market kept by Goanese, who subsequently moved southward to a lane named Dukargully, where they are still to be found.

Duncan Road.[30] *(From Bellasis Road to Erskine Road and Falkland Road.)*

Named after Jonathan Duncan (1756-1811), Governor of Bombay from 1795 to 1811; it is one of the oldest roads in Bombay. The Duncan Causeway (Sion), the Duncan Dock (Government Dockyard in Fort), and Duncan Market, which formerly existed in Shaik Memon Street, are all named after this Governor.

One of the nameplates in Duncan Road is inscribed "Duncon Street".

Durgadevi Street. *(From Duncan Road to Trimbak Purashram Street.)*

Named after the temple of the Hindu goddess Durgadevi, situated in this street. Durga is a name of the goddess Parvati, the consort of Shiva.

Duxbury Lane. *(Colaba Road.)*

Named after J. R. Duxbury, Traffic Manager, and B.B.&C.I. Railway. He entered that Company's service, 1866, and died in July 1892. He lived in Colaba and for many years represented that and the Fort Ward in the Corporation.

Dwarkadas Street. *(From Modi Street to Bora Bazar Street.)*

Formerly known as Devji Dwarkadas Street.

Dyeing Mill Gully. *(From Mahim Bazaar Road to Seashore.)*

Named after a Dyeing Mill situated here.

Eldon Road. *(From University Road to Esplanade Road.)*

Named after Lord Eldon (1751-1838), Lord Chancellor from 1801 to 1827. The lane is close to the Law Courts and many lawyers have offices in it; hence presumably, by the association of ideas, it was named after a great legal luminary.

Elephanta.

"An island in Bombay harbour, the native name of which is Gharapuri (or sometimes, it would seem, shortly, Puri) famous for its magnificent excavated temple, considered by Burgess to date after the middle of the 8th century. The name was given by the Portuguese from the life-size figure of an elephant, hewn from an isolated mass of trap-rock, which formerly stood in the lower part of the island, not far from the usual landing place. This figure fell down many years ago and was often said to have disappeared. But it actually lay in *situ* till 1864-5, when (on the suggestion of the late Mr. W. E. Frere) it was removed by Dr. (later Sir) George Birdwood to the Victoria Gardens at Bombay, in order to save the relic from destruction. The elephant had originally a smaller figure on its back." (*Hobson-Jobson*). It was re-erected in Victoria Gardens in 1914 by Mr. P. R. Cadell, I.C.S., then Municipal Commissioner, and the late Mr. B. H. Hewett, Mechanical Engineer to the Municipality. (*See also* Mori Road.)

Elphinstone Circle.[31] *(Opposite Town Hall.)*

See also Cotton Green.

"This circle of buildings was projected during Lord Elphinstone's Governorship by C. Forjett and with his support and also his successor Frere's it was ready in 1863." (*Maclean's Guide*, 1899, p. 231).

"Also called Amliagal 'in front of the tamarind', the bullock driver's name for Elphinstone Circle from the old tamarind at the North-East corner of the Cathedral close." (Campbell, III, 595.)

Elphinstone road *(from the north end of DeLisle road to Parel road)*

Also is called after Lord Elphinstone, who was Governor of Bombay, 1853 to 1860.

Erskine Road. *(From Falkland and Duncan Roads to Parel Road).*

So named after James Claudius Erskine (1821-93), first Director of Public Instruction, 1854-9; Judge of High Court, 1862-3; and Member of Council, 1865-7. He was the grandson of Sir James Mackintosh. The Indian public call this Null Bazar Road. (q. v.)

Esplanade Road.[32] *(From Esplanade Cross Road to Colaba Causeway.)*

Not much of the Esplanade survives. In 1851 the author of *Life in Bombay and the neighbouring out-stations* (p. 36) was able to write of it as follows: "The Esplanade is a large level space, formerly covered with cocoa-nut trees, but now totally unconscious of any symptom of vegetation, beyond the green turf, with which it is carpeted. An excellent road, of about two miles in length, runs through the centre of it, affording an agreeable drive from the harbour on one side, to the commencement of the native bazaars on the other, and running in a parallel line between the Fort and Back Bay."

Falkland Road. *(From Corner of Null Bazaar to Tardea Tram Terminus.)*

Constructed between 1866 and 1868 (Michael, History of Municipality, p. 408). Called after the tenth Viscount Falkland (1803-84), Governor of Bombay from 1848 to 1853. He was

Governor of Nova Scotia (1840-46), Captain of the Yeomen of the Guard (1846-48). He married a daughter of William IV and Mrs. Jordan, whose book *Chow-Chow* gives a valuable description of life and society in Bombay during her time.

Fanaswadi Lane. *(From Dady Shet Agiary Street to Thakurdwar Road).*
Fanaswadi, Jackfruit garden: (more commonly Phanaswadi).

Fazul Road. *(From Cuffe Parade to Wodehouse Road).*
Named after Sir Fazulbhoy Currimbhoy Ebrahim, Kt., (b. 1872) second son of Sir Currimbhoy Ebrahim, Bart., and owner of house property in this road.

Fergusson Road.[33] *(From DeLisle Road to Worli Road.)*
Named after Sir James Fergusson, sixth Bart (1832-1907) who was Governor of Bombay from 1880 to 1885. He entered the Grenadier Guards in 1851 and served in the Crimea. M.P. for Ayrshire 1854, 1857, and 1865. Under-Secretary of State for India, 1866-67. Governor of S. Australia, 1868, of New Zealand, 1873-75. Under-Secretary for Foreign Affairs, 1886-91. Postmaster General, 1891-92.

Flagstaff Hill. *(See Golanji Hill.)*

Fofalwadi. *(Blind Lane from Bhukshwar.)*
Named after the areca catechu trees that formerly existed here. It is from this tree that there is obtained the famous masticatory best known as betel-nut, which in Persian is called *Pupal* and in Arabic *fufal*.

Foras Road.[34] *(From Bellasis Road to Grant Road Junction.)*
Da Cunha discusses this word at length. Sir Michael Westropp had in a judgment stated that "*foras* is derived from the Portuguese word *fora* (Latin *foras* from *foris*, a door) signifying outside".

Da Cunha disputes that and says that if *fors* (quit rent payable to the King or Lord of the Manor) is to be traced to a Latin origin, it is more appropriate to derive it *forum*, a public place where such affairs as the payment of rents were transacted.

P. P. M. Malabari, in *Bombay in the Making* (p. 388) has the following note : "The roads from the Fort crossing the 'Flats or Foras lands' between Malabar Hill and Parel, were generally known as the 'Foras Roads'; but this general title seems to have been superseded by other names, though this the ancient term is still preserved in a road called the Foras Road."

Mr. P. R. Cadell writes: "Was not the term intended to be applied to roads which were to be constructed by foras – tenure holders? There was long a Foras road shown on the maps, but never constructed, near Elphinstone Road. It is still shown on the large Government map as Proposed Foras Road."

Forbes Street.[35] *(From Apollo Street to Esplanade Road.)*
Named after Mr. J. A. Forbes who was President of the Municipal Corporation, 1874-75. The offices of the firm of Forbes are situated there.

Forjett Street. *(From Gowalia Tank Road to Tardea Road.)*
"So named in memory of an officer of the Bombay Police who, at the time of the Mutiny, by his foresight and extraordinary knowledge of the vernacular saved Bombay from a mutiny of the garrison (Bombay City Gazetteer, Vol. I, p. 43). Charles Forjett (1808-1890) was Commissioner (then styled Superintendent) of Police, 1855-64. Also Chief Municipal Commissioner for Bombay. How to be nipped the Mutiny in Bombay in the bud be himself related in his book *Our Real Danger in India* (Cassell, 1878)."

Fort Chapel. (*See* Convent Street.)

Fort Street.[36] *(From Frere Road to Hornby Road.)*
Probably from Fort George or St. George (on site of St.George's Hospital) of which a few remains survive close by.

French Bridge and French Road (*From Girgaum Road to Queen's Road, including the French Bridge.)*

The Bridge and the road were constructed, 1866, (*Bombay City Gazetteer*, Vol. I., p. 509, gives date wrongly as 1886) and take their name from Col. P. T. French, one of the original founders of the B.B.&C.I. Railway. He was Chairman of the Board of Directors for nearly 32 years and resigned in 1885.

Frere Road.[37] (*From Mint Road to Malet Road.)*

Named after Sir Bartle Frere, first Bart. (1815-1884). Governor of Bombay (1862 to 1867). He came to India in the Civil Service in 1834. Chief Commissioner in Sind, 1850-59. Member of the Council of India, 1867-77. Governor of the Cape, 1878-80.

Fuller Road. (*From Esplanade Road to Mayo Road.)*

Named after Colonel J.A.Fuller, R.E.Superintending Engineer, P.W.D. He was an architectural Engineer and Surveyor, and several of the great buildings in Bombay, such as the Law Courts, were designed by him and constructed under his supervision.

Gaiwadi Gully. (*From Lady Jamsetji Road to Mahim bazaar road.)*

Gaiwadi means literally an open space for cows. There are one or two Gaiwadis elsewhere, e.g., between Girgaum Road and Kalbadevi in the district known as Cavel.

Gamdevi Road. (*From Gowalia Tank to Chaupati.)*

"The Gamdevi temple is considered to be one of the oldest in Bombay. As its name indicates, it is dedicated to the village goddess of that part of the island where it is situated. Gamdevi is derived from *grama* in Sanskrit or *gav* in Marathi, a village, and *devi* a goddess." (da Cunha, p. 55.)

Garden Lane. (*Between Khetwady Main Road and Sandhurst Road.)*

Constructed by the Improvement Trust close to one of their gardens.

Garibdas Street. *(From Dariasthan Street to DeSouza Street.)*

Garibdas means "your humble servant" or "the slave of the poor" and appears to be a singularly infelicitous title for a Bombay landlord to own.

Gell Street. *(From Gilder Street to Ripon Road and Morland Road Junction.)*

A recently constructed road which leads to a police accommodation scheme and is therefore named after a former Police Commissioner, H. G. Gell, M.V.O., Police Commissioner, Bombay, 1904 to 1909.

Ghellabhoy Street. *(From Ripon Road to Mahomedan Street.)*

So named after Ghellabhai Doolubdas, a vakil or pleader, who owned a large portion of the land round about Ripon Road in the district of Madanpura. He still holds the Fazandar rights over some land, but most of the land has been taken up by the Improvement Trust.

Ghoga Street. *(From Parsi Bazaar Street to Hornby Road.)*

The well known Banaji family had property here and the street was so named after the nickname of the family among Parsis—Ghoga. It is said that this nickname was first applied to Cawasji, the father of the famous Framji Cowasji Banaji because he once had an altercation in his shop with a sailor and told him in a loud voice to leave his shop emphatically uttering "Go, Go." The sailor left his shop but standing close by had his revenge by dissuading customers from entering the shop by saying, "Don't go to this 'Go Go's shop." The name caught on and the family is still known among Parsis by this name (Vacha, *Bombay Bahar*, p. 330). Mr. S. M. Edwardes writes:

"Might it not also be named after the place Gogha on the west coast of India? In the early days of British trade the names

Diu, Gogha or Gogo, and Cambay constantly appears. *Cf.* Goghari Moholla. Gogo was the method of spelling Gogha in old records." Mr. Karkaria remarks: "This is not likely because the street was inhabited from the first by Parsis who had no connection with Gogo in Bhavnagar and because the Gujarati name Ghogano Moholla, the street of Ghoga or in which Ghoga lived, is pretty decisive. Moreover, the house in which Cowasji Ghoga or Banaji lived for a long time still exists."

This street had another name until lately, i.e., Tod Street, from James Tod, Head of the Bombay Police, 1779-90, who had his house and chowky here. Tod was afterward removed for bribery (*vide* R. P. Karkaria in the *Bombay Gazette*, 1907, Oct. 7). (*See also* Gunbow Street.)

Ghorupdeo Road. *(From Reay Road to the Junction of Mount Road and Tank Bunder Road.)*

Named after the temple of the goddess Ghorupdevi situated on the road.

Gibbs Road (Malabar Hill). *(From Gowalia Tank Road to Ridge Road.)*

Named after James Gibbs, C.S.I. (1825-1886), Vice-Chancellor of the University of Bombay, 1870-1879, Judge of the High Court, Member of Council, Bombay (1874-79) and Member of Supreme Council (1880-85). Gibbs long resided in a bungalow (now occupied by Mrs. H. A. Wadia) near All Saints' Church, and this road was called after him when it was built in 1879.

Gilder Street. *(From Arthur Road to Grant Road.)*

Named after a public-spirited missionary, the Rev. Charles Gilder who appears to have been held in high regard by the people of Bombay. He was for several years connected with Trinity Chapel and was Secretary of the Indo-British Institution. He survived to about 1895 but seems to have been little known during his later years. (It is now part of Lamington Road.)

Girgaum Road.[38] *(From the junction of Carnac and Esplanade Roads to Gamdevi Road, including the Kennedy Bridge.)*

"From *giri* (a hill) and *grama* (a village), from its situation at the base of Malabar Hill. Another derivation is from *gidh*, from the Sanskrit *Gridhra* (a vulture) and *grama* or vulture village, from the presence of vultures at the Towers of Silence to the north-west of Girgaum. But this is evidently a later derivation, subsequent to the advent of the Parsis to Bombay. The former, that of the mountainous village, seems to be yet true one." (da Cunha, p. 56.)

Goghari Moholla and Lane. *(From Gogari Mohola to Pinjrapole Road.)*

Named after people (mostly Mahomedans) from Ghoga, near Bhavnagar in Kathiawar, who lived here.

Gola Lane. *(From Jijibhoy Dadabhoy Lane to Jiwaji Lane.)*

Also called "Golwad" or the quarter of the Golas. It is occupied chiefly by Parsis now, but Golas used to live there. They are a low Hindu tribe found in Gujarat and also in Bombay. There were many of them formerly. In 1780 there were 102 Golas (Edwardes: *Rise of Bombay*, p. 211). They generally do the work of rice pounding. (About this caste and their habits, etc., vide *Bombay Gazetteer*, Vol. IX, part I, pp. 182-5. Also R. P. Karkaria on Barber Lane in *Bombay Gazette*, 7th Oct. 1907.)

Golangi Hill.

Campbell (*Bombay Town and Island Materials*, III, 648) writes: "Across the Muddy Tank Bunder foreshore and the coal heaps of Frere Bandar stands the quarried face of Brae hill, and the Jubilee, Indo-Chinese, and National Mills, clustered at the foot of the woody slopes of Golangi or Flagstaff Hill."

Gopi Tank Gully. *(From Lady Jamsetji Road to Matunga Road Station.)*

Many tanks are called after the Gopis, or milk-maids of Gokul-Vrandawan, the abode of the god Krishna's childhood. Krishna was so pleased with their staunch devotion to God that all the Gopis of Gokul were able to get Mukti or salvation. In memory of Shri Krishna and the Gopis, pious Hindus name tanks after the Gopis. There is, for example, a Gopi Talao in Surat.

Government Gate Road. *(See Parel Government Gate Road.)*

Governor's Row.

The name is applied by Maclean (*Guide to Bombay*, p. 223) to the part of Churchgate Street, which divides the Oval from the Marine Lines Maidan. The Governors in question whose statues are here are Sir Richard Temple, Lord Reay, and Lord Sandhurst, all on the south side of this "Row".

The first named statue is a landmark recognized in particular by the volunteers, as the following extract from the Bombay Volunteer Rifles' Orders (December 1914) shows: "The Battalion will parade as strong as possible for Battalion Drill at Sir Richard Temple's statue at 4-30 p.m., on Saturday, December 5th."

Gowalia Tank Road[39] *(Cumballa Hill). (From Gamdevi and Tardeo Road junctions to Warden and Nepean Sea Road Junction.)*

Gowalia, cow-herd. The tank, recently filled in, was so named either because herds of cows and cattle came there for water or because gowalias used to collect together there for their midday meal, while the cows were grazing on the hill. It is an old road dating from the eighteenth century.

Grant Road.[40] *(From Grant Road Bridge to Duncan Road.)*

"Constructed about 1840 during Mr. Grant's Governorship at

a time when its surroundings were practically open country."
(*Bombay City Gazetteer*, Vol. I, p. 40.) That date is too late for
Sir Robert Grant was Governor from 1835 to 1838 and the
Gazetteer states elsewhere (Vol. I, 363)—on the authority of
The Bombay Times of Oct. 19, 1839, that on the 1st October 1839,
Grant Road "from the obelisk to the Garden house of Jagannath
Shankar Sett at Girgaum" was thrown open to the public, and
was described as requiring a parapet-wall on either side owing to
its great elevation above the adjoining lands. Sir Robert Grant
(1779-1838) was the son of Charles Grant, a famous Director of
the East India Company and brother of Lord Glenalg, President
of the Board of Control, 1830-34. He died at Dapuri, Poona, in
1838 during his Governorship.

Besides this road, there are other places reminding the citizen
of Bombay of this Governor, e.g., Grant's Buildings at Colaba,
and the Grant Medical College. Douglas (*Glimpses of Old Bombay*,
p. 125) writes: "The Tanna and Colaba Causeways are his
monuments, besides hundreds of miles of good roads between
this and Sholapore."

Green Street. *(From Apolh Street to Custom House Road.)*
Vide Cotton Green.

Gunbow Street. *(From Hornby Road to Bazaar Gate Street.)*

"The curious name Gunbow is probably a corruption of Ganba,
the name of an ancestor of Mr. Jagannath Shankarset. Old
records show that Ganbasett or Genba Shet settled in Bombay
during the first quarter of the eighteenth century and founded a
mercantile business within the Fort walls." (*Bombay City Gazetteer*,
Vol. I, p. 33.)

Another explanation is that the street is called after a certain
Gunbava's well to which, though partly rilled in, offerings of
flowers and cocoanuts are still made. According to common
belief, Gunbava was an ascetic who had his seat near the well.
Bava (father), or Baba among Mahomedans, seems to be an

honorific word.

Another greatly venerated well is a little to the south of Gunbava's and is known as Murgabava's well. It is in a house in Ghoga Street and hence the eastern part of that street as known as Murga seri, or lane.

Gun Carriage Street. *(From Thomas Street to Gun Carriage Factory.)*

The factory was moved from what is now known as Hornby Road to Colaba about 1820.

Ganeshwadi. *(A blind lane from Sheik Memon Street.)*

Named after the temple of Ganpati, or Ganesh, situated in this lane.

Gunga Baodi Road. *(From Gunpowder Road to Dockyard Road.)*

There is a well in this road called Gunga Baodi. *Gunga* (the Ganges in English) is the name the Hindus give to any sheet of water they regard as sacred, besides calling rivers by it. *Baodi* is "a well with steps leading down to the surface of the water." Hindi from Sanskrit *wapi*: intermediate forms are found in *woo, waodi* and *baodi*. More commonly *baoli* or *baori* (*Whitworth's Anglo-Indian Dictionary.*)

Mr. R. P. Karkaria writes: "Another derivation given by Borne to me here refers to a woman called Gunga (this is a common name for Hindu females) who fell into this well being misled by the spirit of the well who has a reputation for playing such pranks. In the vernacular language 'Ganga baodi' would mean 'The woman Ganga is drowned', the cry of the people on the occasion. I was told that this well is noted for the virtue of its water, which virtue was derived from a Brahman pilgrim pouring into it a lota or vessel of water he had brought with him from the Ganges at Benares."

Gunpowder Road. *(From Mazagon Tram Terminus to Reay Road.)*

Named after the powder magazine there.

Guzar Street. *(From Duncan Road to Parel Road.)*

Formerly known as Makund Goojar Sett Street. Gujars or Guzars are inhabitants of Gujarat.

Guzri Bazaar Lane. *(From Parel Road to Chambhar Lane.)*

Guzri in Guzarati means bazar so that the name of the lane appears to be tautologous.

Gymnasium Road. *(From Hornby Road to the North of the Times of India Offices.)*

Named after the Sir D. M. Petit Gymnasium to which it leads.

Haines Road.[41] *(From Parel Road and Clare Road to Fergusson Road.)*

Constructed in 1868 (Michael, *History of Bombay Municipality*, p. 408) possibly called after Sir Fred. Paul Haines (1819-1909). Commander-in-Chief in India (1876-81) though his connection with Bombay is not very obvious.

Hamal Street. *(From Colaba Road to Gun Carriage and goes Southwards to Pestonji Street.)*

This and another street of the same name near Dhobi Talao are called after hamals, meaning palanquin bearers. Fifty years ago palanquins were still common conveyances in Bombay.

Hammam Street. *(From Medows Street to Apollo Street.)*

"Hamam" means "bath" and the street is so called, because there were baths there, somewhere near the entrance to the Share Bazaar. There is, or was, a Hummum's Hotel and Coffee House in London also named from "hamam". "It is so called from an eastern word signifying baths"—(Leigh Hunt's *The Town*, p. 322.)

Church Gate

Lamington Road

Hancock Bridge.

Named after Lt. Col. H. F. Hancock, who was a member of the Municipal Corporation for some years and its President, 1877-78.

Hansraj Lane. *(A blind lane from Love Lane to the East of the Byculla Bridge.)*

There is here a Hindu Temple of the same name. Both the lane and the temple are named after a wealthy Hindu, Hansraj.

Harkness Road.[42] *(From Nepean Sea Road to Ridge Road.)*

Named after Dr. John Harkness, first Principal of Elphinstone College (1835-1862), who had a bungalow there. He died in 1870.

Harvey Road.[43] *(Improvement Trust Scheme IV.)*

A letter from the Municipal Commissioner (Mr. P. R. Cadell) to the Corporation, dated 19th October 1911, says: "With reference to the road which it is proposed to call Harvey Road, Mr. Sheppard in his No. 6470 of 7th June 1909, proposed to call this New Gamdevi Road. The Corporation, in their Resolution No. 1968 of 8th July 1909, suggested that it should be called 'Gamdevi Back Road' or some other name. I do not think it should be called Gamdevi Back Road, for the simple reason that it is not a Back Road, but the portion of an important road leading from the junction of the Gowalia Tank, Grant Road and Girgaum Road to the sea at Chaupati. I venture to suggest that the whole of this road should be called Harvey Road after the former Municipal Commissioner whose name, I think the Corporation will agree, should be commemorated in the city. The name Gamdevi Road would, in that case, be confined to the portion of the Old Gamdevi Road which lies outside the straight road."

Mr. W. L. Harvey (1863-1910) was Municipal Commissioner (1898-1905).

Mr. W. D. Sheppard, I.C.S., Municipal Commissioner, 1905-10.

Hasali Tank Gully. *(From Lady Jamsetji Road to Mogal Gully.)*

Mr. R. P. Masani writes: "Hasali tank is named after Hasalai village. The locality opposite the tank, bounded on the north and on the east by Lady Jamsetji Road, on the south by Portuguese Church Street, and on the west by Bhandar gully, was known as Hasali village. It seems the Bhandaries who came to the locality originally from Tanjira, an island which according to the Gazetteers was also called Habsan, i.e., the Habshi's or African's land, were called Habsani. Their village came to be gradually known as Habsali, a corruption of Habsani, and then as Hasali. I am told that a lane in the locality was also popularly known as Habsali gully and Mr. Kashinath Dhuru (late Chief Inspector of Water-works) says that at one time the locality was mentioned as Hasali in the bills that were preferred by the Water Department in respect of water supplied to the houses in the neighbourhood."

Henry Road. *(From Colaba Causeway to Merewether Road.)*

Named after the late Captain George Fitzgerald Henry of the P.&0. Company. A tablet on Pedder Market Fountain in Mazagon reads as follows: "Presented to the City of Bombay by members of the P.&0.S/.Co.'s service being raised by them as a memorial of Captain G. F. Henry, an energetic citizen and a friend whom in life they regarded with esteem and whose sudden death they deeply deplore. G. F. Henry of the P.&0.S.N.Co., a commander of their ships and their Superintendent afterward for many years at Bombay. Bom in Dublin in 1822, when driving to the office he was thrown from his carriage in the near neighbourhood of this spot and died within two hours. Feb. 23, 1877."

Captain Henry was President of the Municipal Corporation when it was first constituted in 1873, and Chairman, of the Town Council in 1876.

Hermitage Pass. *(From Gowalia Tank Road to Pedder Road.)*

Named after a Bungalow of the same name in this Pass, which

was once occupied by Sir Charles Chambers (1789-1828), Judge of the Supreme Court, who died there, and afterward by Dr. H. Douglas (1821-75), Bishop of Bombay, 1868 to 1874. Vishwanath Mandlik (1833-89), a celebrated Hindu jurist, afterward purchased the Bungalow and resided there.

Hog Island.

"I see that I am credited in the Bombay Gazetteer with the statement that it was so called because ships were careened or hogged there. This will do until some better reason is given. The Hydraulic Lift does not enhance this view of the subject, and I await with patience the resumption of the careening business, so that the truth of this theory may be substantiated, as from present appearances the said interpretation of the name of Hog Island is rather at a discount. We must therefore either change the name or resume business." (Douglas, *Bombay and Western India*, Vol. II, p. 262). The New Oxford Dictionary gives various quotations showing that to hog a ship used to be a good nautical expression. But it is equally probable that the name Hog is here only a term in physical geography. Mr. Weekley in his book on *Surnames* (p. 310) says that Hogg is a nickname, a variant of Hough, i.e., hill, which again is a variant of Hugh or How. As analogies, he cites Cape la Hogue and the hillock called Hooghe at the point of the famous Ypres salient.

Home Street.[44] (From Waudby Road to Hornby Road.)

Homji Street. (From Elphinstone Circle to Gunbow Street.)

An old street, named after Behramji Homji (died about 1750), a rich Parsi Merchant, who with his brother Nasurwanji (died about 1756) founded the well known Dady or Dadysett family of the Parsis, so-called after Nasurwanji's son Dady Nasurwanji (1735-1799). As a banker, the latter was widely known and is mentioned in several Memoirs of that time (e.g., Admiral Garden's *Autobiography*, p. 190, Hove's *Tours in Gujarat*, etc.). Homji and his family after him long resided in this street.

Hope Street. *(From Fuller Road to Esplanade Road.)*

Named after the late T. C. Hope (1831-1915) who was Municipal Commissioner for a short time, January to May 1872. After a career in Bombay, he became Secretary to the Government of India in the Finance and Commerce Department, 1881-2, and for a time Finance Member in 1882.

Hormusji Street. *(From Gun Carriage Street to Colaba Road.)*

Named after Hormusji Cooper, a well-known Army Contractor, who had property here.

Hornby Road.[45] *(From Carnac Road to Church Gate Street.)*

Named after William Hornby, Governor of Bombay, from 1771 to 1784.

It was called Hornby Row at the time when it only extended as far north as Bori Bunder. The road from Bori Bunder to Crawford Market was at first known as Market Road but is now part of Hornby Road. "Row" seems to have slipped imperceptibly into "Road". Mr. P. R. Cadell when Municipal Commissioner tried to restore the former term but was not successful.

Hornby Vellard. *(From Clerk Road to Love Grove Road.)*

Vellard, from the Portuguese *vallado*, a fence or embankment, is said to be peculiar to the island of Bombay, and now is used only in this one connexion—the name Hornby Vellard being as often as not abbreviated into "The Vellard". That its use was at one time more common may be seen from the fact that Maria Graham (in 1809) refers to the Sion Causeway as a vellard. Whitworth's Anglo-Indian Dictionary suggests that the Marathi *walrad*, to cross over, would supply a derivation as *vellard* may be met with under the form *walade*.

Hornby should be obvious enough but commentators will not admit the simplicity. Hobson-Jobson—which apparently confuses the Hornby Vellard with the Sion Causeway—

points out that the former seems to have been built some 20 years before Hornby's time and refers the reader to Douglas, *Bombay and Western India*. Douglas, however, only points out the discrepancy. Mr. Karkaria explains that this was due to the fact that a causeway over the Breach was built before Hornby's time but had been destroyed by the sea. Hornby rebuilt it on a much stronger basis and for this heavy expenditure, the Court of Directors censured him. The chief authorities seem to be:

(1) Buist's *Guide to Bombay* (1851or1852) puts the date of construction about 20 years before Hornby's governorship. Thus: "Traditions still exist to the effect that the sea flowed from the west up to the former of these (Paidhoni) until excluded by the embankment from Mahaluxmee to Love Grove constructed above a century ago" (i.e., 1752). Elsewhere the same authority says the Vellard, which he calls Love Grove. Vellard was built in Governor Hornby's time betwixt 1776 and 1780.

Grose (*Voyage*, Vol. I., p. 52) writes in 1750: "The causeway at the Breach where the sea had so gained on the land as nearly to divide the island."

(2) Maclean's *Guide to Bombay* (p.11 of 22nd edition) says: "The construction (in Governor Hornby's time, 1771 to 1784) of the vellard closing the main breach of the sea, from Mahaluxmee to Love Grove, made a great change in the appearance of the island." Maclean adds the story, reproduced in the *Bombay City Gazetteer* (Vol. II., p.121), that Hornby built the vellard without the sanction of the Court of Directors.

One other point has to be mentioned. The causeway itself seems for some time to have been called by the name of the breach it closed. "The Great Breach a name given by perversion of terms to a long causeway which excludes the sea from the low lands of Bombay." (*Bombay Quarterly Review*, April 1856.) This use of the word "breach" survives in Breach Candy. "Breach Candy seems to mean the beach at the mouth of the hollow or pass, that is to say, the hollow between Cumballa ridge on the north and the Malabar ridge on the south. The use of breach for wave-breaking or surf, the modern beach, is common among writers of the sixteenth and seventeenth centuries. By the middle of the eighteenth century the word seems in Bombay to have been locally applied to the break or gap in the rocks of the western shore, through which the sea flooded the Flats: while Candy is the old spelling of Khind or Pass, as exemplified by Sir James Mackintosh's Ganesh Candy (1804) for Ganesh Khind. The absence of either a tower or creek at this point militates against Dr. Murray Mitchell's derivation from Buraj-Khadi (the creek tower)." (*Bombay City Gazetteer*, Vol. I., p. 28.)

The Gazetteer's explanation of what Breach Candy connotes is that which is generally accepted, i.e., its northern boundary would be about Mahaluxmi temple. But this does not appear always to have been the case, for da Cunha (p. 57) writes: "The bridge over the 'wide breach of land' is now called Breach Candy. It is also called Vellard." He then, without apparently noticing the discrepancy, goes on to give the explanation (from Campbell) which is quoted in the Gazetteer and given above. Major H. A. Newell's *Guide to Bombay* (published in 1915) also identifies the Hornby Vellard with Breach Candy.

Many of the letters from Robert Brown quoted in *Passages in the life of an Indian Merchant* (published in 1866) are dated from "The Breach", (i.e., the bungalow which still stands at the end of Warden Road where it joins the Vellard) others are headed "Breach Candy". One letter, dated Breach Candy, 19th May 1854, begins: "I have just escaped from the dining room to Mr. Candy's old room." Mr. Candy there referred to is apparently the well-known S. P. G. Missionary who came to Bombay in 1836, and it seemed quite possible that his name was perpetuated in the place-name. Unfortunately for that theory, the name Breach Candy is found in advertisements at any rate as early as 1828.

Hospital Lane. *(From Esplanade Road to Marine Lines.)*
Named after the Military Hospital in this Lane.

Hospital Lane. *(From Be Lima Street to 726 feet eastwards.)*

Named after the Police Hospital that formerly existed here.

Hughes Dry Dock.

Named after Sir Walter Hughes, C.I.E., born 1850, Chairman of the Bombay Port Trust from 1892-98 and again 1900-10. Also, first Chairman of the City Improvement Trust when it was constituted, 1898. Knighted on the occasion of Prince of Wales's visit to Bombay, 1905-6.

Hughes Road.[46] *(From the junction of Gibbs, Pedder and Gowalia Tank Roads to Chaupati Bridge; opened in 1908.)*

Named after Sir Walter Hughes in recognition of his services to the Improvement Trust. To him was due to the Improvement Trust Act, and he was the first Chairman of the Trust. (*See* Hughes Dry Dock.)

"The melancholy example of Hughes road which some have already converted into Hugis Road." (*The Times of India*, 11th May, 1911.)

Husenkhan Khalifa Street. *(From Carnac Road to Janjihar Street.)*

Huzria Street. *(From Grant Road to Bellasis Road.)*

The name is possibly from *hujra,* a room set apart for a holy person, in fact, a prophet's chamber. There are two tombs of holy men in the street.

Imamwada Road. *(From Parel Road to West Jail Road.)*

Imambarah is a building in which the festival of the Mohorrum is celebrated and taziahs or shrines preserved. (Whitworth's *Anglo-Indian Dictionary*, p. 128.) This Imamwada or *bara* of the Shiah Mahomedans plays a great part during the Mohorrum festival in Bombay and is over 100 years old.

Isaji Street. *(From Bhandari Street to Samuel Street.)*
See note on Samuel Street.

Islampura Street. *(From Khetwadi Main Road to Falkland Road.)*
It is principally inhabited by Mahomedans (Islam), Pura or para means a quarter of a town: Islampura—the quarter inhabited by Mahomedans.

Israel Moholla. *(From Musjid Bunder Road to Tantanpura Street.)*
"Israel Moholla and Khadak in Mandvi represent the places to which they (the Bene-Israel community in Bombay) moved before finally settling in Umarkhadi." (*Bombay City Gazetteer*, Vol. I., p.249.)

Itola Street. *(From Argyle Road to Musjid Station Road.)*
Constructed by the Bombay Port Trust in 1883, and named after the city of Itola in Gujarat, near Baroda, on the B.B.&C.I. Railway.

Jackeria Musjid Road. *(From Masjid Bunder Road to New Bengalpura Street.)*
So called after a mosque there built by a Memon merchant named Haji Jackeria (corresponding to the Jewish name Zachariah), who was well known in Bombay; in the early part of the nineteenth century. Lutfullah (1802) mentions him in his *Autobiography* where he says he put up in Jackeria's Mosque when he came to Bombay in 1823: "I put up in a mosque called Haji Zachariah's Musjid. Here I was treated by the servants of the Haji himself with respect and hospitality. I wished to have the pleasure of seeing the founder of this mosque, the Haji, of whose benevolent character I had heard much whilst in Bombay; and on inquiry, I was informed by his servant, who waited on me, that the Haji often sat and talked with me after prayers. Indeed, I recollected a man has done so but never taking him for that great man I always slighted and despised him. I regretted much having

been so rude to a man who treated me with hospitality, yet could not but imputes part of the blame to his own rude dress and manners. It is, however, incumbent on me to apologize for the past, I repaired to his office, where I found him squatted down on an old cushion spread on the floor, with an old bolster pillow behind his back, whilst his servants and attendants being smartly dressed, every one of them excelled his master in appearance. There were also English gentlemen, a captain, and his second officer, belonging to one of his ships, standing there, hat in hand, perhaps for his orders. These were going to be given when I arrived. I was received with much civility and seated next to him. I begged pardon for having unintentionally slighted him in his former visits to me, which I assured him was owing to ignorance of his station. He replied bluntly, that being made of humble dust his duty was to be humble.

I then asked him to furnish me with a passport, as without such security from a person of consequence nobody could go out of Bombay at that time. Upon this he told me to take my oath that I was not imposing upon him in this matter; and on my having done so he ordered his people to give me one, which being immediately written out was signed by him and delivered over to me. I then having offered my thanks to him returned home to the mosque." *Autobiography of Lutfullah*, Ed. by E. B. Eastwick (1857), pp. 210-212.

Jacob's Circle[47] *(Ripon Road.)*

"Formerly known as the Central Station, was given its present name in 1886, in honor of General Le Grand Jacob." (*Bombay City Gazetteer*, Vol. I., p.44.) Sir George Le Grand Jacob (1805-81) was a cousin of the famous John Jacob of Jacob's Horse. He was in the Bombay Army and the Political Department. At Kolhapur, during the Mutiny, he rendered signal service by disarming the mutineers of 27th Bombay Native Infantry. He was also a scholar and transcribed the Asoka inscription at Girnar. His adopted daughter gave the handsome fountain which adorns the centre of the Circle through which pass seven roads—"Sat Rasta", a name by which the circle is often known.

Jagonnath Jiwanji's Lane. *(A blind lane from Fanaswadi.)*

Jail Road. *(From Bast Babula Tank Road to Jail Road South.)*

Named after the Dongri Jail situated in this Road.

Jairajbhai Street. *(From Suklaji Street to Foras Road.)*

Named after the late Mr. Jairajbhai Peerbhoy (1832-1887), a member of the Corporation and a leading (Khoja) Mahomedan citizen. He was a wealthy China merchant.

Jambli Street. *(From Carnac Road to Bhandari Street.)*

Jambli Tank Street. *(From Mahim Bazaar Road to Lady Jamsetji Road.)*

Named after Jambul trees. Mr. Kashinath Devji Dhuru, the late Chief Inspector of Water-works, says there were two such trees near the tank, one of which fell down about 60 years ago. The jambul tree *(Eugenia jambolana)* is known all over India for its fruit and is venerated by Buddhists and Hindus.

Janjikar Street. *(From Sheik Memon Street to Dongri Street.)*

Jeejeebhoy Dadabhoy Lane. *(From Suparibag Road to Parel Government Gate Road.)*

Jeejeebhoy Dadabhoy Street. *(From Bohra Bazaar Street to Hornby Road.)*

Named after a Parsi, who owned a large property here— Jeejeebhoy Dadabhoy Mugana (1786-1849). He was the grandfather of the late Mr. Nanabhai Byramji Jijibhai: his surname Mugana was derived from a mute (muga) ancestor. Jeejeebhoy Dadabhoy, born in 1786, died in Bombay, May 1849. He was a well-known banker, broker, and agent. An obituary notice of him in the *Illustrated London News,* August 4, 1849, states: "Jeejibhoy Dadabhoy was one of the most active among the native capitalists in the establishment of the three banks in Bombay, and he served his time as director respectively in the Oriental and Commercial Banks. To him and to Sir Jamsetjee Jeejeebhoy, the inhabitants of Western India are indebted for the introduction of steam navigation for commercial and passenger traffic—the steamer Sir James Rivett Carnac, the first, and by far the best-paying, of the Bombay steamers having been built by them. Jeejibhoy Dadabhoy, the manager of this company, so judiciously conducted the business, that in the course of six years he divided profits amounting to nearly the outlay. ... A temple costing 50,000 rupees, or £5,000 was a few years ago built entirely at his expense: and wherever in the Island of Bombay a well could be dug to supply water to the poor, Jeejibhoy Dadabhoy assisted in the means for the same."

Jetha Street. *(From Gilder Street to Sunderdas Mill Lane.)*
Named after the father of the late Mr. Mulji Jetha. (*See* Mulji Jetha Market).

Jivajee Lane. *(From Gola Lane to Hornby Road.)*
Called after the late Shapurji Jivajee Wacha (1841-1913) son of Jivajee Manockjee Wacha, who formerly owned land in the locality.

Jiwanji Maharaja's Wady. *(A blind lane from 3rd Bhoiwada Lane.)*
Named after a Hindu (Bhattia) High Priest of the same name. A temple bearing his name is in this lane.

Joonda Street. *(Near Kambekar Street, east of Parel Road Bhendi Bazaar.)* .
So called from a Joonda, or flag, which was formerly on the top of a Hindu temple there. Flag and temple have gone, but the locality is still called Nishanpura from this fact. *Nishan*, sign, signal.

Junction Road. *(From Haines Road to Clerk Road.)*
Because it joins Haines Road with Clerk Road, on the west of the B.B.&C.I. Railway at Mahaluxmi Station.

Kair Gully. *(From Old Purbhadevi Road to Dhun Mill, Elphinstone Road.)*
In Marathi *kair* means sweepings, and probably the name is derived from this.

Kakadwadi. *(From Kandewadi Lane to Girgaum Back Road.)*
Presumably from *kakadi*, a cucumber or gourd.

Kalachowki Road. *(From Arthur Road to Reay Road and Sewri Road Junction.)*
Named after the Police Chowki situated at the east end of the Road, which is dammered (pitched) on the outside, and is, therefore, *kala*, black.

Kalbadevi Road. *(From Camac Road to Parel Road.)*
"Earns its title from a shrine of Kali or Kalikadevi, once located in the island of Mahim and removed to this locality during the period of Mussulman dominion." (*Bombay City Gazetteer*, Vol. I., p. 37). The *varia lectio* of Kalkadevi is still common, and in an advertisement in *The Bombay Times* of 1840, it appears as Kulba Davee. The road was very narrow till the beginning of the nineteenth century and the temple of the Goddess Kalba devi (Kalika devi) occupied a large portion of the road. After much negotiation with Raghunath Joshi, the owner of the temple, it was arranged that the site should be acquired for widening the road and that a new temple should be built.

Kalicut Street. *(East of Mint Road.)*
Named after the town of Kalicut in Southern India.

Kalyan Street. *(From Olive Road to Frere Road.)*
Named after the town of Kalyan in the Thana District.

Kalyandas Kriparam Wady. *(A blind lane from Bhuleshwar Road.)*

Named after a Hindu citizen of the same name. This Kalyandas was surnamed Motiwala because his ancestors were pearl *(Moti)* merchants.

Kamathipura.

"Kamathipura, which forms an almost perfect rectangle between Bellasis Road, Duncan Road, Grant Road, and Suklaji Street, was until 1800 liable to periodical flooding by the sea. The section, which earns its title from the Kamathis, a tribe of artizans and labourers who immigrated from H. H. the Nizam's Dominions towards the end of the eighteenth century, contains no building of interest and is occupied for the most part by the lowest classes of the population." *(Bombay City Gazetteer*, Vol. I., p. 44). As a fact, the district could not have been flooded after the construction of the Vellard (see Hornby Vellard) and the streets in it were laid out about 1803. The term Kamathipura is commonly used to denote the prostitutes' quarter, and the same may be said of Grant Road and Suklaji Street, both of which names connote a good deal more than geography.

Kambekar Street. *(From Musjid Bunder Road to New Bengalpura Street.)*

So named after a former landlord who owned property there, a Konkani Mussalman called Kambekar. Nothing further can be discovered about him and the inhabitants in the street do not know anything about him. With them, the name of the Street is *Chhas* Street, from the fact that formerly chhas, whey or skimmed milk, was sold there. At present, there are no such shops in the street.

Kandewadi Lane. *(From Girgaum Back Road to Girgaum Road.)*

Named after the warehouses of onions *(kanda)* that exist here.

Karelwadi. *(From Thakurdwar Road to Girgaum Road.)*
So named because of the sandstone *(karel)* in the locality or after a kind of brick and chunam wall known as karel or karo.

Kasai Street. (North of Sandhurst Road and west of Mutton Street.)
So called from *kasais,* butchers, who generally reside there. They are a distinct class of Sunni Mussulmans, marrying among themselves.

Kasar Gully. *(A blind lane from Girgaum Road.)*
Kasar is the Hindi form of Marathi *Kansar,* from the Sanskrit *kansya.* The name of a high Sudra caste; they are workers in brass and bell-metal, and cover copper vessels with tin. (Whitworth's *Anglo-Indian Dictionary.*)

Kasara Basin Road. *(From Dockyard Road to Coppersmith Street.)*
The basin in the docks must have taken its name from the coppersmith (kasar) community in the neighbourhood. There is Kasar Street in Kalbadevi, where there are many coppersmiths' shops.

Katha Bazaar Road.
So named from there were shops in the locality where *katha* or coir is sold.

Kazi Street. *(From Banian Road to Erskine Road.)*
Named after Kazi Mahomed Londe, one of the Kazis of Bombay Mahomedans. Kazi (Arabic), "A judge. Under the Muhammadan empire, the kazi was a civil and criminal judge. Under British rule, he became an adviser to the courts on points of Muhammadan law. He still holds a high place in Musalman communities and leads the public prayers on great festivities. He is also Registrar of marriages and divorces, for which he receives fees; he has also usually some endowment." (Whitworth's *Anglo-Indian Dictionary.*)

Kazi Sayyad Street. (From Bhandari Street to Samuel Street)

Kelawadi. *(A blind lane from Girgaum Road.)*
So named because banana (*kela*) plantations exist here.

Kennedy Bridge.

Kennedy Sea Face.
Named after Michael Kavanagh Kennedy (1824-1898) who entered the E.I.Co.'s service in the Engineers in Bombay, 1841; Lt.Col. 1861; Secretary to Government of Bombay, P.W.D.1863; K.C.S.I., for services during the famine, 1876-8, in Bombay and Madras; Director-General of Transport during the Afghan War, 1879-80; retired, 1880; Col. Commandant, E.E., 1891.

Khadak Street. *(Mandvi.)*
So named because the soil is rocky, *khadak* meaning rock. The locality, which embraces several streets, is hence called *khadak* by natives.

Khamballa Hotel Lane. *(A blind lane from Gowalia Tank Road to Khamballa Hotel.)*
Named after the Hotel of this name, which at one time enjoyed a considerable reputation. Maclean's *Guide to Bombay* recommended it as the best for a lengthened stay. The Hotel building now forms part of the Parsi General Hospital. Khamballa is a *varia lectio* for Cumballa (see above under that name).

Khambata Lane. *(From Khetwadi Back Road to Falkland Road.)*
Named after Jehangir Dadabhoy Khambata (Engineer) who owned property in this lane.

Khanderao Wadi. *(A blind lane from Dady Shet Agiary Street.)*
Khanderao (Marathi), "The name of an incarnation of Siva. There is a class of persons mentioned by Colebrooke called the

dogs of Khanderao. These are first-born children dedicated to the temple of Khanderao, near Poona, by persons who have, in the hope of obtaining progeny, made vows so to dedicate their first children." (Whitworth's *Anglo-Indian Dictionary*.) Khanderao, or more commonly Khandoba, is an aboriginal god, subsequently accepted by the Brahmans as an incarnation of Siva, to whom both boys and girls are dedicated at his temple in Jejuri (Poona). The girls become prostitutes. They are not necessarily first-born children. (S. M. Edwardes.)

Khandia Street. *(From Grant Road to Undria Street Cross Lane.)*

There was a tank of this name here, possibly from khan meaning "sugar".

Khara Tank Street. *(From Khoja Street to Parel Road.)*

"Khara" means saltish or brackish: the water of this tank, which has been filled up, was not fit for drinking.

Khatau Road. *(From Wodehouse Road to Cuffe Parade.)*

Named after Mr. Goverdhandas Khatau, an owner of house property in this road.

Khatteralli Lane. *(From Thakurdwar Road to Kandewadi Lane.)*

Named so because Khatris, a sect of Hindus, live here. These Khatris claim to be Maratha Kshatriyas (*Khatri* is a Hindi abbreviation of *Kshatriya*): they resemble in dress and appearance the Somavanshi Kshatriyas.

Khetwadi Main Road. *(Cowasji Patel Road to Lamington Road).*

Khetwadi Back Road. *(From Falkland Road to Charni Road.)*

Khet, field. The district was not built over until 1838 when it began to attract residents and it rapidly developed after the construction of Falkland and Charni Roads.

Khoja Street. *(From Erskine Road to Grant Road.)*

Khoja Mahomedans (vide *Bombay Gazetteer*, Vol. IX, pt. 2, pp. 36-50) chiefly inhabit it and they have their Jamatkhana, or communal assembly house, in the locality.

Khoja, or khwajah, is a Persian word. "The title is one of respect applied to various classes: as in India especially to eunuchs: in Persia to wealthy merchants: in Turkistan to persons of sacred families." (*Hobson-Jobson*). But the word has now a different and far more precise connotation. "The Khojas are descended from Hindu converts of Cutch, Gujarat, and Kathiawar, and profess the Shia Muhammadan creed. They form one of the most important and interesting sections of the various races that are permanently located in this city and pay tribute in various forms to the Aga Khan as their spiritual or religious head." (*Bombay City Gazetteer*, I., 181.)

Khotachiwadi. *(From Girgaum Road to Girgaum Back Road.*

The Wadi, or oart, belonging to the *khot*, i.e., lessee of land, "a revenue contractor or farmer. In the Konkan are many hereditary khots who have by degrees assumed many of the rights of proprietors of the land." (Whitworth's *Anglo-Indian Dictionary*.) The khot pays the land tax to Government and then he has the power to sublet the land to others on short or long leases: in most cases, the leases were perpetual leases with conditions that they should last till the chandra surya, i.e., so long as the existence of the Sun and the Moon.

Kika Street. *(From Kalbadevi Road to C. P. Tank Road.)*

Named after a Hindu citizen the late Jagjivan Kika. This street is also vulgarly known as Gulalwadi, the place where a peculiar red powder named gulal, used especially at the Holi festival for sprinkling on people, is sold.

King Lane. *(From Bazaar Gate Street to Gola Lane.)*

Kingsway. *(From the old tramway terminus, Elphinstone Road, to the railway bridge, Sion station.)*
At a meeting of the Bombay Improvement Trust held on 20th April 1911, the Chairman explained the proposed development of the Dadar-Matunga scheme and the gardens proposed to be laid out at the highest point of Vincent Road due east of Matunga station. It was then proposed to ask the King-Emperor to permit this circular garden to be known as "King's Circle" and the avenue from Crawford Market to Sion Causeway as "King's Way". The names have gradually come into use without any explicit authority. The Circle was given its present form in 1916, and Kingsway (now generally written as one word only) has been constructed to its full width of 150 feet for a short length only at its south end, which is not yet Crawford Market but the old tram terminus in Elphinstone Road.

Kitchen Garden Lane. *(From Sheikh Memon Street to Princess Street).*
Named after a vegetable garden that existed here belonging to the East India Company.

Kittredge Road. *(From Colaba Road to Cuffe Parade.)*
Named after Mr. G. A. Kittredge the first promoter and Managing Director of the old Bombay Tramway Company, in consideration of his excellent services to the City. (For the early history of the Company and for details of the contract with Messrs. Stearns and Kittredge, see *Gazetteer*, I., 359.) He was an American citizen and for many years a prominent, philanthropic citizen of Bombay. He with the well-known Sorabji Bengali (1831-1893) took a lead in the movement for bringing out lady doctors for Indian women.

Kochin Street. *(From Frere Road eastwards to a new road along the seashore.)*
Named after the state of Cochin in Southern India.

Kolbhatwadi

Kol Koli (one of the most ancient communities in Bombay) and Bhat, landed estate.

"Some derive it (Koli) from the Sanskrit kola, 'a hog', a term of contempt, applied by the Aryans to the aborigines. Others say that it means 'pig-killer'. Some derive it from the Mundar Horo or koro, which simply means 'man', while others connect it with kol 'a boat', seafaring being their principal occupation. Again, it is said that koli means 'clansman' as he derives his name from kul, 'a clan', just as Kunbi derives his from kutumb, 'a family' and hence is the 'family man'." (da Cunha, p. 40).

Kolsa Street. *(From Nakhoda Street to Parel Road, Bhendi Bazaar.)*

So called because *Kolsa*, coal, is sold there. There are still coal shops in the street, also the houses of coal merchants.

Kompta Street. *(From Mint Road to a new road along the seashore.)*

Named after a town of that name in the Kanara district.

Kumbhartookdi Lane. *(A blind lane from Bhuleshwar Road.)*

Kumbhar means a potter and *tukda* or *tukdi* mean a piece or plot; a plot reserved for potters. In Bombay *tukdi*, or *tukda* means a policeman's beat.

Laburnum Road. *(Improvement Trust Scheme IV, Road 5.)*

Because of the description of the trees planted by the Improvement Trust along this Road in 1911.

Ladiwady. *(A blind lane south of Old Hanuman Lane.)*

Named so from a sect of Hindu Banias called Lad who reside here. "Lads take their name from Lat-desh, the old name for Gujarat." (*Bombay Gazetteer*, Vol. IX, part I, p. 72.)

Lady Hardinge Road.

On September 23, 1914, the Municipal Commissioner (Mr. P. B. Cadell, I.C.S.) reported to the Corporation that the new 60 feet road, constructed from the B. B. & C. I. Railway Matunga Level crossing past Lady Jamsetji Road to Mahim Bazaar Road, "has been completed and will be open to traffic as soon as lamps have been erected. The road is already 3,100 feet long and will ultimately be extended across the two railways and joined to the Improvement Trust Road on the east of the Matunga Station. On the west side, it may ultimately be possible to continue it to the sea. It is thus an already important road and in its present condition is one of the prettiest in Bombay." He thought it would be a suitable perpetuation of the memory of Lady Hardinge's visit to Bombay so shortly before her lamented death if the road were to be named after her and he proposed, therefore, with the sanction of the Corporation, to call the road the "*Lady Hardinge Road.*"

In moving that the road is named Lady Hardinge Road, Sir Bhalchandra Krishna said that it would be a fitting thing to do so, as Lady Hardinge's memory was held so dear in the city.

Lady Hardinge, a daughter of Lord Alington, was born in 1868 and died July 1914: she married Lord Hardinge of Penshurst— Viceroy of India 1911-16—in 1890.

Lady Jamsetji Road.[48] *(From Junction of Dadar Road and Portuguese Church Street to Mahim Causeway.)*

Named after the wife of the first Sir Jamsetji Jijibhai (1783-1859). She built the causeway, called after her "Lady Jamsetji Causeway", to which this road leads. The causeway, now generally known as Mahim causeway, was opened in 1845 and was described as "a stupendous mound which cuts off an arm of the sea and promises to give to the husbandman what has hitherto been an unproductive estuary, a bridge which enables the travelers to pass a dangerous ferry in safety." (*Gazetteer*, II. 155.)

There is a legend, lately brought to light again in *The Bombay East Indian*, that the causeway was built by Lady Jamsetji in fulfillment of a vow made to our Lady of the Mount, Bandra. That there is no foundation for this was shown by Mr. Karkaria in a letter published in *The Advocate of India*, September 22, 1910. He says the idea of building the causeway "had long floated before the mind of several leading citizens of Bombay and a member of the Wadia family had actually offered to Government a sum of money which was, however, found inadequate for the expenses which the causeway would entail. Another Parsi, a member of the Banaji family, had in 1837 undertaken to raise a fund among wealthy natives for the purpose, but he did not succeed. The immediate cause which led Sir Jamsetji and his lady to undertake this very useful work on their own account was a terrible catastrophe in the Bandra creek when 20 ferry boats capsized and all the passengers and animals on board were drowned. This sad intelligence determined him to bear all the cost of the causeway himself and to build a road, which should in future obviate the necessity for passengers between Bandra and Bombay of crossing the creek in boats. The government also helped to the extent of a quarter of the whole cost which amounted to over two lakhs of rupees. The road leading from the Bandra end of the causeway to Mount Mary where the Chapel is situated was completed in 1854 at the joint expense of the Government and Sir Jamsetji, the latter contributing six thousand rupees."

Lamington Road.[49] *(From Queen's Road to Arthur Road.)*

On May 1, 1913, the Municipal Commissioner (Mr. P. B. Cadell, I.C.S.) informed the Municipal Corporation that the Improvement Trust had constructed a broad road from the end of Queen's Road to Gilder Street. "This runs," he said, "chiefly along the line of the old Depot Lane and Chunam Kiln Street, but a new name is required to cover the whole length of the street which constitutes a most important thoroughfare.

I would suggest for the approval of the Corporation that the street should be called 'Lamington Road'. Lord Lamington, as Governor of Bombay, took a warm interest in the affairs of the city and visited its streets very frequently, and I think it would be a graceful act on the part of the Corporation to associate permanently his name with one of its thoroughfares. I should, in fact, suggest that the name of Lamington Road should also be given to the whole of Gilder Street up to Arthur Road. Gilder Street forms practically one continuous street with the new road and its present name has not any historical and other associations that are worth preserving." On the motion of Sir Pherozeshah Mehta, it was resolved to name it "Lamington Road". The 2nd Baron Lamington, b.1860, was Governor of Bombay, 1903-7.

Land's End Road. *(From Nepean Sea Road to Land's End.)*

(*See* Narayen Dabulkar Road.)

Lansdowne Road. *(From Colaba Causeway to Adam Street.)*
Named after the fifth Marquis of Lansdowne (born 1845) who was the Governor-General of India from 1888-1894.

Lohar Street. *(From Sheikh Memon Street to Princess Road and from Girgaum Road to Queen's Road.)*
Named after the shops of ironmongers (*lohars*) along this street.

Love Grove. *(North of Hornby Vellard and at the South end of Worli Hills.)*
"There is another very pleasant drive across the Vellard (or causeway) to a pretty little promontory bearing the romantic appellation of Love Grove, which is said to have originated in the circumstance of this spot having formerly been selected as the grand resort of newly married couples during the honeymoon. Nor was it inappropriately chosen; for before the construction of the Vellard rendered it so easy of access to all the world, the seclusion was as complete as even the Arabian desert could

offer." (*Life in Bombay and the Neighbouring Outstations*, 1851.)

In a chapter entitled "Bombay—circa 1839" (*Bombay and Western India*, I. 189) Douglas writes: "Most of the English merchants of this period lived at Mazagon. One now or shortly after had an elegant residence at Love Grove, Worli, with a big banian-tree in the garden, on which he had inscribed Milton's famous lines, in which he describes this trophy of Dekhan vegetation."

Love Grove has been deprived of its romantic associations by sewers, drains, pumping stations and other accessories of the worst smell in Bombay.

"When the Government of Bombay is again searching for someone whom the King may delight to honor, we hope they will single out the individual in the service of the Bombay Corporation who is responsible for our street nomenclature. Apparently, he prefers to blush unseen, for no one knows who he is, but he is a genius of the highest order. One of his gems is the delectable title of a small lane near Girgaum, which used to rejoice in the distinct appellation of 'Night Soil Depot Lane'.

That is a nice savoury and suggestive address heading...But more recently this gentleman has gone a step farther. Realizing that the bumpy lane past the Pumping Station, which is the despair of motorists and an olfactory outrage on every passer-by, should not remain undistinguished, he has christened it 'Worli Love Grove Pumping Station Road'...It is a pity that so much bright ingenuity should stop short here, and as the descriptive art is to be cultivated in our street nomenclature, we suggest a few alternative titles to the Commissioner. What could be more appropriate than 'Road to the Ten Thousand Unnecessary Stinks', for any new thoroughfare in the neighbourhood of Love Grove? Or 'Road Guaranteed to Cure the Most Sluggish Liver', which would aptly describe the last section of Lady Jamsetji Road before it joins Bandora Causeway? Or 'Road which ought to have Been Widened Fifty Years Ago' for Old Purbhadevi Road?"(*The Times of India*, February 1911).

Love Lane. (From Mount Road to Parel Road.)

Low-Level Road North of Falkland Road Overbridge.

Since this little book was begun the above mouthful has been condensed to Falkland Bridge North, and similar changes have been made in the names of various other low-level roads. But the lengthy form of nomenclature or rather of topographical definition is still common in Bombay (see above under Love GRove) and appears to be spreading to the districts. At Thana, for instance, may be noted "Koliwada on the other side of the Railway".

Lukhmidas Market.

Named after Lakhmidas Khimji (1830-1901), a prominent Bhatia merchant and reformer. This market was recently partially burnt down.

Madanpura. *(The district through which Ripon Road passes.)*

It is named after Madan, or Madoo, a well known Mahomedan from Allahabad who settled here two generations ago and owned land much of which came after him into the hands of Ghellabhai *(q.v.)*. Madan was of the *Julhai* or weaver caste and was a weaver by profession. "The Musalman hand-weavers known as Julhais or Jolahas congregate in Madanpura between the Ripon and Morland Roads." (*Bombay City Gazetteer*, I, 200).

Magdala Road. *(From Colaba Road to Beach Road.)*

Obviously called after Magdala, the Capital of Abyssinia, which was stormed in 1868. But why? (1) Perhaps to commemorate the main achievement of an expedition that had been fitted out in Bombay. (2) In compliment to Lord Napier of Magdala who had been Commander-in-Chief, Bombay (1865-69), before becoming C.in C.Or (3) After one of the two turret ships (the "Magdala" and the "Abyssinia") bought in 1871 for the new Naval Defence Squadron. These ships were stationed in Bombay harbour.

Mahadeo Shankar Sett Lane. *(A blind lane from Sonapur Street.)*

Mahaluxmi Street. *(From the north side of Argyle Road to south side of Argyle Road.)*

Named after a cotton mill of this name in the street.

Mahaluxmi Temple Lane. *(From Warden Road to Mahaluxmi Temple Compound.)*

Named after the famous temple of the goddess *Mahaluxmi.*

(For the curious legend of this particular Mahaluxmi, see K. Eaghunathji's *Hindu Temples*, No. 64, pp. 17-24, and *Gazetteer*, III, 356.)

Mahim.

"Mahim is undoubtedly the Portuguese equivalent of Mahikavati, the pompous Sanskritised form of Mahi meaning either the earth or the Great (Goddess) which was the name given to the island by Bhimdeo's colonists. Fryer mentions it in 1698 under the name of Maijm. Downing calls it Mayam in 1737; while Murphy states that in ancient Marathi histories of Bombay Mahim is referred to as Bimbasthan, Prabhawati, and Mahikavati." (*Bombay City Gazetteer*, p.29.)

Mahim Bazaar Road. *(From Old Purbhadevi Road to Lady Jamsetji Road.)*

The Corporation was asked in 1916 to change the name to Cadell Road, "in view of the many activities of Mr. P. R. Cadell, C.I.E., I.C.S. (Municipal Commissioner, 1910-1916) and because the old name has become meaningless as the Bazaar is now of no consequence." It is not quite the case that the name had become meaningless for the Bazaar is still important. But the Corporation in deciding on the change included in the proposed Cadell Road not only Mahim Bazaar Road but also Bhandarwada Road and Jambli Tank Road.

Mahomedan Street. *(From Ripon Road Westward.)*

This street is on land formerly owned by Ghellabhai *(q.v.)* who settled here, with many Mahomedans from the North-West (now the U. P.). Hence it's name.

Malabar Hill.

"But why Malabar? The coast of Malabar does not begin until you proceed as far south as Coorg. We suspect that Fryer himself gives us its derivation in describing the tank at the end of it, when he says that it was to bathe in it 'the Malabars visit it most for', a place of pilgrimage in fact, to which came people of the coasts south of Bombay, who were all then lumped together under the generic name of Malabars. Hence Malabar Hill. Not quite satisfactory, you say? Of all things, the most perplexing is the origin of names. The old lady in our Cathedral had no such perplexity. On seeing the tomb of General Carnac, Clive's second in command, at the battle of Plassey, and knowing well what a power the name of Carnac had been in Western India for the last hundred years—"Dear me," she exclaimed, "then that's the origin of the word Carnatic?" (Douglas, *Round About Bombay*, p. 66.)

The Hill—the native name of which is Sri Gundi, which seems to mean "Lucky Stone"—is also said to derive its name from the fact that the neighbourhood of the Walkeshwar temple on it was a favourite haunt of the Malabar pirates.

"Shri-Gundi is called Malabar Point after the pirates of Dharmapatan, Kotta, and Porka on the Malabar Coast, who, at the beginning of British rule in Bombay, used to lie in wait for the northern fleet in the still water in the sea of the north end of Back Bay. In 1668 so exposed was the trade of Bombay to Malabar pirates and to Shivaji that three small armed ships had to be built as convoys." (*Bombay Gazetteer. Materials*, Part III, p. 667.)

Malet Bunder.

So named after Arthur Malet (1806-1888), the brother of Hugh

Pointz Malet (1808-1906), the discoverer of Matheran. He was in the Bombay Civil Service from 1826 to 1860 and was a member of Council from 1855 to 1860. Arthur's Seat, Mahableshwar, is also named after him. He took a great interest in the project for wet and dry docks in Bombay.

Malharrao Wadi. *(A blind Lane from Dady Shet Agiary Street.)*

Mandlik Road. *(From Colaba Causeway to Merewether Road.)*

After the late Rao Sahib Vishvanath Narayan Mandlik (1833-89), a distinguished Konkanasth Brahman from Ratnagiri, who became Government Pleader in Bombay, 1884. He was for many years a member of the local as well as the supreme Legislative Councils. He published a large work on Hindu law and owned a paper '*Native Opinion*'.

Mandvi

Mandvi, which is written Mandovim in Portuguese documents and Mandavie in early English records, is the ordinary Marathi word for a Customs House. (*Bombay City Gazetteer*, 1, 26.)

Manekji Street. *(From Bora Cross Lane to Nowroji Road.)*

Called after the late Manekji Mistri. "He had a house there which, though it has changed hands, is still known as Manekji Mistri's house. I remember having seen the old proprietor." (Communicated by Shams-ul-Ulma Jivanji Jamshedji Modi.)

Mangaldas Road. *(Improvement Trust Scheme II, Road 7, 1911.)*

On the east of this road is the Mangaldas Cloth Market which was the property of Sir Mangaldas Nathubhai, Kt., (1832-90), a wealthy Kapole Bania citizen, who was a large benefactor to the University and helped several charitable institutions. Also a member of the Legislative Council, Bombay. He was the great-grandson of Manordas Rupji Dhanji (1727-92). (*See also* Manordas Street.)

Mangalore Street. *(From Frere Road to a new Road along the seashore.)*
Named after the town of Mangalore in Southern India.

Mangelwadi. *(A blind Lane from Girgaum Road.)*
Named after a fisherman caste of Hindus called *Mangelas* who used to live there.

Mangesh Senoy Street. *(From Fort Street to Bora Bazaar Street.)*

Manordas Street. *(From Bora Bazaar to Mint Road.)*
Named after Manordas Rupji Dhanji (1727-92), a wealthy Bania Hindu banker and merchant. His father Rupji Dhunji was a native of Gogha near Diu in Kathiawar and he was one of the earliest of his caste of traders to settle in Bombay where he supplied goods to the Company's Government. Manordas was highly respected by his people and became "Nagarseth", or Seth, or lord of the City, amongst them—a sort of Lord Mayor in his caste, an office long continued in his family. He was the great-grandfather of Sir Mangaldas Nathubhai, Kt., (1832-90), and of Verjiwandas Madhowdas, both distinguished Kapole Bania citizens of Bombay. The latter was the father of Sir Jagmohandas Verjiwandas, Kt. Rupji Dhanji—the ancestor of the families of Sir Mangaldas, Sir Harkeshandas, and Sir Jagmohandas—was an inhabitant of Gogha, who settled in Bombay in 1656.

Manson Road.
Called after Mr. George Manson, who was Secretary to the Port Trust Board from its formation in June 1873 to March 1890.

Marine Lines. *(Facing Queen's Road. From the Junction of Wellington Street and 1st Marine Street to Church Gate Street.)*
Named after the barracks of the Marine Battalion situated here.

Of the various lanes in the neighbourhood, Third Marine Lane is sometimes known as Vaniawadi, because Hindus of the Vania caste formerly lived there: but they have gone and it is now inhabited by Parsis. Fourth Marine Lane is known as Gowliwadi, after the *gowli*s (milkmen) who used to have stables there.

Marine Street. *(From Customs House Road to Apollo Street.)*

Market Road. *(From Hornby Road to Paltan Road.)*
On account of its situation on the south of the Arthur Crawford Market.

From Bori Bunder to the Crawford Market (now part of Hornby Road) was formerly known as Market Road.

Maruti Lane (Fulgully). *(A blind Lane from Bhuleshwar Street.)*
Named after the Hindu temple of the god "*Maruti*".

"*Maruta* (Sanskrit) Wind, a god of the wind. The Marutas are Vedic gods or demi-gods; they are described as being the sons and brothers of Indra, also as children of the ocean, sons of heaven armed with lightning and thunderbolts." (Whitworth's *Anglo-Indian Dictionary*.) Mr. S. M. Edwardes writes: "This seems to me wrong. The god *Maruti* has nothing to do with the Vedic Maruts. *Maruti* is another name for *Hanuman* the Monkey-god, a very popular god among the lower classes."

Matarpakhadi Road. *(From Mazagaon Road to Reay Road.)*
Among the old residents of Bombay, like the Somavanshi Kshatriyas or Panchkalshis, *Mhatr*e is a surname. *Mhatra* means an elder or a superior person and as the locality was occupied by the Mahtre families it was called the *Pakhadi*, or quarter, of the *Mhatras*.

Mathew Road *(From Girgaum Road to Queen's Road.)*
Named after Francis Mathew, the late Agent and Chief Engineer, B.B.& C.I. Railway.

Matunga Road. *(From the Junction of Sion and Vincent Roads to Leper Asylum.)*

Named after the village of Matunga in Bombay. "*Matunga* was perhaps *Matanga Ali*, or *Matangasthan*, which would mean either the place of elephants or the place of the *Mhangs*. As regards the former it is the merest conjecture that Bhimdeo, or Bimb Raja, may have stationed his elephants in this locality while he was the ruler of Mahim; while the latter meaning is discountenanced by the fact that early writers never spoke of the low castes of Bombay by this appellation." (*Bombay City Gazetteer*, I., 29.)

Mayo Road.[50] *(From Esplanade Road near Queen's Statue to the junction of Esplanade Road and Wodehouse Road.)*

Named after the sixth Earl of Mayo (1822-1872), Governor General of India from 1869 to 1872. M. P., 1847-67 and Chief Secretary for Ireland in three administrations. Murdered at Port Blair, Andaman Islands, Feb. 2, 1872.

Mazagaon Road. *(From Jail Road east to Mount Road.)*

"Mazagaon is possibly a corruption of Machcha-grama (Fish-village) in allusion to the large colony of Koli fisherfolk who settled there in pre-historic times. The name is variously spelled Mazaguao by the Portuguese and Massegoung by early English writers and has been defined by some to be Mahishgrama (the buffalo-village) and by others to mean the central village on the analogy of the Marathi Mazaghar (the central portion of a house). The last derivation is the most plausible." (*Bombay City Gazetteer*, I., p.27.)

Medows Street.[51] *(From Esplanade Road to Forbes Street.)*

Named after General Sir William Medows, who was Governor of Bombay and Commanders-in-Chief, Bombay, 1788-1790. He occupied the quarters assigned to the then Commander-in-Chief, namely, a large house at the corner of Medows Street. Few names are more commonly misspelled. It is not uncommon to see printed stationery used by shopkeepers in the street on which Medows has been turned into Meadows or Meadow. Sixty years ago the Bombay Almanack used invariably to spell the name Medow, and this spelling appears in Mrs. Allen Harker's admirable novel *Jan and her job* published in 1917.

Memonwada Road. *(From Jail Road to Bkajipala Street.)*

This place is chiefly inhabited by Memons. "The Memons (i.e. Muamins or Believers) are converted to Islam from the Lohana and Cutch Bania castes. . . .when they first commenced to do business in Bombay at the opening of the nineteenth century they appear to have opened tailoring establishments in Lohar Chawl, which was then known to the police as the thieves bazaar." (*Bombay City Gazetteer*, I., 178.)

Merewether Road. *(From Yacht Club Chambers to Arthur Basin.)*

Named after a former Chairman of the Bombay Port Trust (Oct. 1880—May 1892) Colonel G. L. C. Merewether, R.E.

Messent Road.

In a letter to the Corporation presented in July 1917, the Municipal Commissioner recommended the naming of the road constructed by the Port Trust on the Mazagaon-Sewri Reclamation after their Chief Engineer Mr. P. G. Messent, CLE. The Corporation adopted the recommendation that the road is named "Messent Road". Mr. P. G. Messent, b. 1862, has been Chief Engineer to the Port Trust since 1899, having been Assistant Engineer 1884-1899. He had carried out the Alexandra Dock and the Hughes Dry Dock work. He received the C.I.E. In 1914,

Mewawala Lane. *(From 1st Cooper Street to Parel Road.)*

"In Bhendi Bazaar there is an Agiari opposite the stables, the scene of the Mahomedan riots in February 1874. It was built by Bomanji M. Mewawala, or fruit man, in 1851." (da Cunha p. 298.)

Military Square Lane. *(From Medows Street to Esplanade Road.)*

Named so because in this lane were situated the offices of the Military Department and Harbour Defences.

Milk Street. *(Between Byculla Station Road and Tank Pakhady Street.)*

Constructed by the Improvement Trust on an estate largely devoted to buffalo stables. The Hon. Mr. J. P. Orr writes: "In our debate about naming small streets near the buffalo stables in East Agripada it was thought that the names should indicate the uses of these large stable blocks. 'Buffalo Street' was rejected as cacophonous: 'Milk Street' was accepted as harmless: and then some wag suggested 'Water Street' and that was accepted as appropriately allusive to the malpractices of *gaulis*."

Mint Road. *(From Fort Street to Elphinstone Circle.)*

Named after the Bombay Mint premises situated on this road. "The erection of the present Mint was sanctioned by the East India Company in 1823, and an inscription on the building shows that it was designed and constructed by Major John Hawkins of the Bombay Engineers, was commenced in 1824 and completed in 1829." (*Bombay City Gazetteer*, III., p. 306.)

Mirchi-Market Lane. *(From Sheik Memon Street to Janjiker Street.)*

On account of the *Mirchi* (chilli) market in this lane.

Mirza Street. *(From Abdul Rehman Street to Sheik Memon Street).*

Flora Fountain

Victoria Station

Mirza Ali Street. *(North of Imamwada Road.)*

Mirza Ali Mahomed Khan, a Persian, was a prominent citizen and a member of the old Board of Justices. He owned property in this locality.

Mody Street. *(From Fort Street to Barrack Street.)*

Named so on account of Modikhana (Commissariat Stores) situated at the south end of the street. Modi (in Hindi) a grain dealer and grocer; a village shop-keeper. In Bengal, the Mahajan is chiefly the wholesale and the modi the retail dealer. (Whitworth's *Anglo-Indian Dictionary*.)

Morarji Gokuldas Cloth Market. *(Kalbadevi Road.)*

So named after Morarji Gokuldas (1834-1880), a wealthy Bhattia merchant and public-spirited citizen, who was at the time of his early death in 1880 Member of the Bombay Legislative Council. This cloth market was erected about ten years ago by his sons and called after him.

Mori Road. *(From the B. B. & C. I. Railway Level Crossing near Mahim Station to Lady Jamsetji Road.)*

"Named so because the street was flanked by houses owned by Moris, a class of Marathas. These Moris appear in all probability to be the descendants of the Mauryas who ruled over the Konkan in early times and whose capital was the town of Puri, which was called the Goddess of Fortune of the Western Sea. The Konkan Mauryas are supposed to be a branch of the Maurya dynasty of Pataliputra (Patna) which was founded by Chandragupta (Sandracotas of Alexander) in the fourth century B.C. The existence of the Mori locality in Bombay Island and of the Mori Bandar close to the Bombay Harbour goes to strengthen the belief that the Puri of the Mauryas and of the Silaharas of the Konkan was the Island of Ghara-Puri or Elephanta. The Mauryas were followers of Buddhism and many Buddhistic relics have been discovered at Elephanta." (Communicated by a correspondent).

Commenting on the above Mr. S. M. Edwardes writes: "I think it would be more correct to say that More or Mori is a surname common among certain of the lower classes in Bombay, e. g. the Kolis, and is evidently a corruption of Maurya, just as Cholke, another surname, is a corruption of Chalukya, and in evidence of the power which the Maurya dynasty once exercised over Bombay. I think it more likely that the Mauryan Puri was not Elephanta, but Thana. I never heard of Buddhistic relics at Elephanta. On the other hand, obvious relics of Hinduism have been found there. It is not certain that the Konkan Mauryas were followers of Buddhism like Asoka."

Morland Road. *(From Bellasis Road to Ripon Road.)*
Named after the late Sir Henry Morland, Kt., born 1837, served in the Indian Navy and the Indian Marine; Port Officer, Bombay, Chairman of the Corporation in 1886; Knighted 1887; died 1891.

Motlibai Street. *(From Souter Street junction to Gell Street.)*
Named after the Parsi philanthropist lady Motlibai Nowroji Wadia (1811-1897). She was the mother of N. N. Wadia (1837-1907) who founded the famous Wadia Trust Fund of a crore of rupees.

Mount Pakhadi Lane. *(From Mount Road to Tank Bunder Road.)*
Mount Pakhadi is one of those curious compounds from two languages that are common in place-names all over India. Pakhadi means a district or quarter.

Mount Pleasant Road. *(From Ridge Road to Nepean Sea Road.)*

Mount Road. *(From Mazagon Road to the Junction of Tank Bunder and Ghorupdeo Roads.)*

Mugbhat Street. (*From Girgaum Road to Khandewadi Lane.*)

Named after the little shrine of Mugbhat, said to be derived from the name of a Koli named Munga, and bhat, which means a landed estate in the dialect of the Kolis, just as Kolabhat, or Colaba, means the land of the Kolis. (da Cunha, p. 64.)

Rao Bahadur P. B. Joshi suggests that this locality was called Mugbhat on account of its being used for the cultivation of the grain called muga, or *Phaseolus mungo.* All the neighbouring streets or localities are named after the trees, fruits, or plantations that were produced or existed there, *e.g.,* Phanaswadi from the garden of jack trees, Kelewadi from the plantain garden, and Pimpalwadi from the pipal trees which still abound in that street and so forth. The suggestion immediately lands the inquirer in a botanical puzzle. *Phaseolus mungo* is a kind of pulse known in the vernacular as *udid* or *urd;* another variety Phaseolus radiatus is the plant known in the vernacular as mung. (Watts, *Commercial Products of India,* p. 881.) How does muga or mugh come into use?

Mujavar Pakhadi Road. (*Mazagon.*)

So named from *Mujavar* meaning in Arabic a keeper or guardian of a Mahomedan mosque or a saint's tomb. *Pakhadi* means a locality. There were formerly some Mahomedan tombs in the locality, which was thus called after their *Mujavar.*

Mulji Jetha Market.

Mulji Jetha was a Hindu merchant who built this market for wholesale cloth business, as well as, in 1875, the Lakshmi Narayen temple in Kalbadevi Road for the use of Hindus from Gujarat.

Mumbadevi Road. (*From Sheik Memon Street to Kalbadevi Road.*)

There are two traditions connected with the foundation of the Mumbadevi temple. The first tells us that more than five hundred years ago a Koli fisherman by name Munga erected a temple on the Esplanade and called it *Mungachi Amba*, which was contracted into Devi Mumbai or Mumbai. This temple was removed to near Pydhoni, in about 1737, as the place on the Esplanade was required by Government. There is also another tradition which is connected with the mythical giant Mumbaraka who harassed the worshippers of the temple and is supposed to be the Pathan King of Delhi Mubaraka. (da Cunha, p. 45.) The above account does not appear to be correct for we find the name Mambai in records prior to the invasion of Mubarak. The Goddess *Mumba or Mah-Amba* and her temple existed long before Mubarak, and she is believed by local Hindus to be same as *Mah-Amba*, or Durga, and her puja is performed the same day as that of Durga. (Vide App. to *Early History of Bombay*, by P. B. Joshi.)

After commenting upon the connection between the King Mombaros, mentioned by the author of the Periplus of the Erythrean Sea (A.D. 247; McCrindle, 113), and Bombay, Sir James Campbell gives his final decision that Mumba is a special form of *Maha Amma*, the Great Mother, designed to glorify the local guardian by embedding in her name a trace of the defeated Mubarak Shah. It is, however, possible that the name is a corruption of *Maha-Amba-ai* (the Great Mother Amba), *Amba* being a synonym of Parvati, wife of Siva, and the suffix "*Ai*", meaning "mother", being a term of respect often applied by Marathi-speaking Hindus to their goddesses. This view is corroborated by the fact that the Hindus, even of today, speak of the city as "Mambai" or "Mumbai". Other authorities, however, consider that this derivation is not phonetically possible and trace the origin of the name to *Mommai*, the title of a village-goddess in Kathiawar." (*Bombay City Gazetteer*, I. 24.)

Murzban Road. *(From Connon Road to Ravelin Street.)*
Named after Khan Bahadur Muncherji C. Murzban, C.I.E. (Born 1838) who has a house in the vicinity. He was in the P. W. D. from 1857 to 1893 when he became Executive Engineer to the

Municipality. In 1890-91 he was President of the Corporation and in 1906 was Sheriff of Bombay. Murzban is a Persian word and originally meant a guardian of the frontiers, a name given to the "lords of the marches" under the Sassanian Empire. Mr. Murzban derives his family name from his great-grandfather Murzban Kaoos Munjam (1763-1822) the founder of the family.

Musjid Bridge. *(From Dongri Street to Argyle Road.)*

Musjid Bunder Road[52] **(Mandvi**). *(From Mumbadevi Road to Dongri Street.)*

Musjid Station Road. *(From Argyle Road to Clive 1st Cross Road.)*
Named after the Musjid Station of the G.I.P. Railway to which it leads.

Musjid Street. *(From Bapoo Khote Street to Parel Road.)*
So named from the mosque called Nawab's Musjid, situated at the East end of the street, which was built by Nawab Aiyaz of the Mysore family of Tipu Sultan who was brought to Bombay in the last century. He lived at Mazagon where he built a tank, called after him Nawab Tank. Near this tank is a bridge on the new Harbour Railway called Nawab Tank Bridge.

Mustan Tank Road. *(From Huzria Street to Tank Street.)*
Named after the tank of the same name recently filled in. The tank derives its name from a Mahomedan saint, Syed Mustan Shah Kadri, who came to Bombay about a century ago, from Hama near Baghdad and from Pishin near Kandahar and whose tomb is near the Tank. Mr. Karkaria learned in the neighbourhood that the saint was here in the time of Baji Rao II., the last Peshwa.

Mutton Street. *(From 1st Duncan Road Cross Lane to Grant Road.)*
Named after the old Mutton and Fish Market, part of the Null Bazaar near Erskine and Duncan roads. This and the

neighbouring vegetable Market "were unpaved and consisted merely of a few ranges of low narrow sheds surrounded by a rough wooden palisade." (Michael, *History of the Municipal Corporation*, p. 479.) This street is generally known as Chor Bazaar Street from *Chor* meaning "thief", as stolen goods are supposed to be brought there for sale.

Nagdevi Street. *(From Carnac Road to Chunam Kiln Street.)*

"Owes its name to an old shrine of the serpent." (*Bombay City Gazetteer*, I, 35.)

Nag, or Naga (Sanskrit)—a snake, particularly the naia tripudiens or cobra di capello. Also, the name of fabulous serpent demons with human faces, supposed to reside in *patal* (Whitworth's *Anglo-Indian Dictionary*.) It is a common belief that the nether regions are inhabited by a species of semidivine beings, half-men half serpents, called *Nag*s. In the Puranas are a number of mythological traditions concerning them.

Naigaum Road. *(From Wadala Road to Bhoiwada Night Soil Depot.)*

Nayagaum is a corruption of the name Nyaya gram or nyaya gaun. According to tradition Bhima Raja's palace and the court of justice were situated in this locality. Fortunately, there are here still a few faint traces and relics of Bhima Raja's period or remembrance. The site of his palace is still pointed out in the oart called the Chimanlal Maharaja's Wadi. Broken relics of ancient times, such as the image of Shiwa, Ganpati, and other articles found by Deoji Patil of Bhoiwadi, who was employed to supervise the excavation work for the foundation of the Maharaja's Bungalow, built there some thirty or forty years ago, are still lying in the Maharaja's Oart and Bungalow. This is a place worth visiting with some knowledgeable person such as the hereditary priest of the place, or some old inhabitant. Deoji Patil was an intelligent Bhoi-Agri and possessed a good deal of information about the locality and about the followers of Bhima Raja. (Communicated by Rao Bahadur P. B. Joshi.)

Nakhoda Street. *(From Nagdevi Street to Abdul Rehman Street.)*

Nakhoda (Persian *nakhuda*) means a skipper, the master of a native vessel. Perhaps the original sense is rather the owner of the ship, going with it as his own supercargo. (*Hobson-Jobson.*) In this case, nakhoda is said to be derived from the well-known family of Nakhoda Mahomed Ali Roghay (1848-1910), the first Mahomedan member of the Legislative Council nominated by Government and one of the first members of the Bombay Presidency Association. His father repaired and enlarged the Jama Mosque in 1837. The family still has a house in the street but the old family house is now the Market Post Office.

Nall Bazaar Market.

"Opened in 1867 and so called from the fact that the main drain of the city flowed past this point in earlier times on its way to the sluices at Varli." (*Bombay City Gazetteer*, I, 41.)

Nullah, a corruption of the Hindi *nala*, a ravine, a gutter, or a drain.

Nanabhoy Byramji Oart. *(From Queen's Road to Wellington Street.)*

Named after Nanabhoy Byramji Jeejeebhoy (born Nov. 1841, died Feb. 1914), son of Byramji Jeejeebhoy, C.S.I. He joined first the firm of Messrs. George S. King and Co. in 1865, and when this firm ceased to exist in 1873, Mr. Nanabhoy still retained the Agency of Messrs. James Burton and Sons, of Manchester, which business he carried on till 1883. He was made a Justice of the Peace in the year 1869, and a fellow of the University of Bombay in 1872. He was elected by Government a Director of the Government Savings Bank and he served as a member of the Board of Accounts of the University for several years. The government also appointed him a member of the Factory Commission which sat in Bombay in 1884 under the presidency of Mr. W. B. Mullock, C.S. He served on the local committees of several exhibitions. Mr. Nanabhoy was a member of the

Corporation from the time of its formation. Bombay owes him a debt of gratitude for breaking down, with the late Mr. Forbes, the ice monopoly held by Tudor & Co., and for organising fetes in honour of Indian troops returned from the Afghan War and the Egyptian campaign of 1882. (*The Times of India*, February 9, 1914.)

Nanabhoy Lane. *(From Cawasji Patel Street to Hornby Road and Churchgate Street.)*

This lane was formerly called Nanabhoy Framji Lane after Nanabhoy Framji Banaji or Davur (1798-1837), a prominent Parsi merchant whose family owned property there and whose ancestral Agiary or fire-temple founded in 1709 and called Banaji's Agiary is still situated in it. In 1887 a kinsman of Nanabhoy Framji Banaji and a trustee of Banaji's Agiary Nanabhai Dhanjibhai Banaji (1842-1900) greatly improved this lane by widening it and in several other ways and the Municipality re-named it after him, but the name was shortened to Nanabhoy Lane. Another lane in the Fort, a little to the north of it, has a similar name, Nanabhoy Bomanji Lane *(q.v.)* from which it is to be distinguished.

Nanabhoy Bomanji Lane. *(North of Gunbow Street.)*

Named after Nanabhoy Bomanji Sethna, a large Parsi landed proprietor of the latter half of the eighteenth century. He was the brother of Muncherji Bomanji Sethna (1712-1799) after whom an Agiary or fire-temple near Khara Talao, Shaikh Memon Street, is named. (*Vide* Agiary Lane from Shaikh Memon Street to Dhanji Street.)

Naoroji Fardoonji Road. *(From Colaba Causeway to Adam Street Seashore.)*

Named, by the Municipality, in 1897, after Naoroji Fardoonji (1817-1885), a well-known Parsi citizen who was called "The Tribune of the people" on account of his long and anxious watch over their interests in the Municipality and Legislative

Council. In early life, he accompanied Sir Alex Burnes to Kabul as Native Secretary and Translator but returned to Bombay before the Afghan War broke out in 1838. From 1845 to 1864 he was employed in the Supreme Court as Interpreter. He went thrice to England on political missions, the last time as a witness before the Fawcett Committee on Indian Expenditure in 1873. He was also a zealous Parsi reformer and took a prominent part in several movements for social and religious reform. He was also Secretary of the Parsi Law Association and laboured hard to obtain separate legislation for his community. C.I.E. 1884. (*Buckland Ind. Biog. Dictionary*, pp. 157-8.)

Naoroji Hill.
"This hill, of which the Sett families are proprietors and which contains their ancestral mansion at its highest point, is the original Dongri Hill, upon which a fortress was erected during the early years of British dominion and whence the Sidi, Admiral of the great Mughal, on one occasion battered the English castle and fortifications." (*Bombay City Gazetteer*, I., 36.)

Naoroji Rustomji Sett (born 1662, died 1732) was the first Parsi who went to England in 1724; he there settled a large money dispute which the Company's officers here had decided against him and obtained a sum of five lakhs and a half from the London authorities. The hill may have been called after him by his son Maneckji Naoroji to whom it was alienated. The history of the hill and of other parts of the Old Portuguese Mazagon estate of the Tavora family is given by Da Cunha (p. 221 et. seq) though not with great clearness. In Portuguese days the bill was known as Vezry hill. It has now been acquired by the City Improvement Trust.

Napier Road. *(From Colaba Road to Beach Road.)*

Napier Road. *(From Esplanade Road to Hornby Road.)*
From the juxtaposition of the first of these roads with Magdala Road (q.v.) and of the second with Outram Road (q.v.) it seems

clear that the first is called after Lord Napier of Magdala (1810-1890) who was Commander-in-Chief, Bombay, 1865-9, during which time he commanded the Abyssinian Expedition; and that the second Napier Road is called after Sir Charles James Napier (1782-1853). Bombay took sides very warmly in the historic controversy between him and Outram about the necessity for the conquest of Sind and the question of the treatment of the Amirs.

Narayan Dabulkar Road. *(From Nepean Sea Road to Land's End.)*

Called after the Hon. Narayan Vasudeo, a well-known Hindu resident of Bombay and a Member of Council. His family originally came from Dabul, a sea-port in the Ratnagiri district, hence the surname Dabulkar. He was born in 1833 and died from fracture of the skull as the result of the collapse of his bungalow situated in this road in August 1874. More often known as Land's End Road on account of its position on the extreme north-west of the Malabar Hill promontory.

Narayan Dhuru Street. *(From Nagdevi Cross Lane to Paidhowni Road.)*

Named after the Dhuru family which is included among the old Hindu residents of Bombay. Members of this family possess large estates in Girgaum and at Dadar, Mahim, etc. They are Suryavanshis and many members of this caste work as gardeners and cultivators.

Narelwadi Lane. *(Mazagon.)*

The land belongs to a Parsi named Narielwala. The founder of the family, Naoroji Cowasji Narielwala (1757-1825), at first traded in coconuts (*nariels*) and later became a wealthy China merchant. In 1822 he built a fire-temple at Mazagon (Narielwala's Agiary) which was moved in 1901 to Dadar.

Naska Tank Gully. *(From Lady Jamsetji Road to Gopi Tank.)*

Named after the tank of the same name. Naska in Marathi

means spoilt; the water of this tank was spoilt and unfit for human consumption.

Navi Wadi. *(Blind Lane from Dadyshett Agiary Lane.)*
Navi—new. So called by the Prabhus who migrated to the locality from other parts of the town.

Nawab Tank Road. *(From De Lima Street to Matarpakhadi Road.)*
Named after Nawab Aiyaz of the Mysore family of Tipu Sultan. (*Vide* Musjid Street.)

Nepean Road.[53] *(From Ridge Road to Nepean Sea Road.)*
Named after Sir Evan Nepean, first Bart., (1751-1822). Governor of Bombay (1812-1819). He entered the Navy as a clerk. Secretary to Lord Shuldram, 1782, Under-Secretary of State in the Shelburne Ministry; Under Secretary for War, 1794; Secretary of the Admiralty, 1795-1804; Baronet,
1802; Chief Secretary for Ireland, 1804.

Nesbit Road. *(From Mazagon Road to Parel Road.)*
So called from Mrs. Rose Nesbit, a Catholic, wife of Commodore Nesbit, Harbour Master of Bombay, under the E. India Company, who had property here. On her ground, she built a private chapel in 1787, with sufficient endowment to support a priest, for whom a small house was added. Before her death in 1819 she gave over the chapel and property to the Vicar Apostolic and her remains were buried in the chapel. The first buildings of St. Mary's Institute was placed close by in 1860 or so, and the chapel was used by the institute till it was replaced by the present church of St. Anne which was consecrated in 1881. Meantime St. Mary's Institute expanded—the large buildings being finished in 1867 and others added later up to the present dimensions. It is now called "St. Mary's High School."

An old tablet in the sacristy of St. Anne's Church bears the following inscription: *Haec ecclesia edificata fuit per Rosam Nesbitt in honorem Sae Anna MDCCLXXXVII.*

New Babulnath Road. *(From Chaupati to Hughes Road.)*
Named after the Hindu Temple of Babulnath. (*Vide* Babulnath.)

New Bengalpura Street. *(From Memonwada Road to Tandel Street.)*
Men from Bengal, chiefly seamen, firemen, and serangs used to live in this and Old Bengalpura Street and a few are still to be found there.

New Dharamsala Road. *(From Sandhurst Road to Dharamsala.)*
So named as a Hindu Dharamsala (rest-house) is situated here. Dharamsala, or Dharamsala, is Hindi from the Sanskrit *Dharma* (that which holds man in the right path, religion, law; or subjectively, virtue, morality, duty) and *sala*, a hall.

New Ghur Lane. *(East of Parel Road.)*

New Hanuman Lane. *(From Kalbadevi Road to Princess Street.)*
There are two Hanuman Lanes: (1) Old Hanuman and (2) New Hanuman Lane. Both of them are called after the temples of the god Hanuman situated therein. (Almost all the houses in these two lanes as well as at Kalbadevi Road were about half a century ago owned by the Yajurvedic Brahmans and the Somavanshi and Suryavanshi Pathares or Prabhus. At present with one or two exceptions most houses there are owned or occupied by Bhatias and other Gujarat people.)

New Nagpada Road. *(From Parel Road to Cursetji Manackji Statue.)*
Named after the temple of the serpent god close by, which is worshipped on Nagpanchmi day, i.e., the fifth day of the Hindu month Shravan.

New Purbhadevi Road. *(From DeLisle Road to Old Purbhadevi Road.)*
Named after the temple of the goddess Purbhadevi.

"Next in importance to Mumbadevi in age and interest is the famous temple of Prabhadevi or Prabhavati, the family goddess of the Patane Prabhus, who may be likened to the Normans of William the Conqueror. The temple is situated at Lower Mahim, a couple of miles to the north-west of the Railway station. The original building was erected some centuries ago at a place called Kotwady, where the remains of an ancient Fort are still visible and was destroyed by the Portuguese." (da Cunha, pp. 47-48.)

New Queen's Road.[54] *(From Queen's Road to Sandhurst Road.)*

Nickdavari East. *(From Kandewadi Lane to Girgaum Road.)*

This lane is called after the Nirgundi or Nikdavani trees (*Vitex negundo* or *Vitex trifolia*) that exist there. This tree is used by the local Hindu residents for purposes of fumigation. Pregnant women and infants are required to take their bath in water in which the Nirgundi leaves are boiled. (Rao Bahadur P. B. Joshi.)

Sir Dietrich Brandis gives, in *Indian Trees* a number of vernacular names for *vitex negundo* but not those mentioned above. Sir G. Watt says the ash of the tree is one of the sources from which is obtained the potash salts employed by the people of India in their arts, science, and medicine.

Nicol Road. *(Off Ballard Road.)*

Messrs. Nicol and Co. were the Managers of the Elphinstone Land and Press Company, originally formed in 1858 for the reclamation of the foreshore, the construction of godowns and the erection of a cotton press. (*Bombay City Gazetteer*, III, 69-70.) The house was long prominent in Bombay, especially as it held the agency of the British India Steam Navigation Co. It is therefore appropriate that a street near the docks should be called after it. The failure of the firm in 1877 was due to the failure of the Glasgow Bank.

Nishanpada Road. *(From Jail Road south to Pydhoni Road.)*

Nishan means a flag and Pada means a village. (*See* Joonda Street.)

Nizam Street. *(From Parel Road to Kazi Street.)*

So called from a former property holder thereof the name of Nizam, a Mussalman from the Konkan.

Northbrook Street. *(From Falkland Road to Bapty Road.)*

Named after Lord Northbrook who was Governor-General of India from 1872 to 1876. Northbrook Gardens were opened in honour of Lord Northbrook when he visited Bombay in November 1872.

Nowland Street. *(From De Lima Street to Church Street.)*

So named after Richard Nowland, a well-known landed proprietor in Mazagon in the latter half of the eighteenth century. He rented from the Company a part of what was then known as the Estate of Mazagon. In a letter to Government, dated 15th September 1779, he calls himself "leaseholder of Mazagon for the term of 99 years". (Forrest, State Paper, *Home Series*, Vol. II, p. 247. Cf. also *Bombay Gazetteer*, Hist. Materials, Part III, 436-446.) He is most probably the Richard Nowlands who is mentioned in Forrest's State Papers (*Home Series*, Vol. I, p. 217), as having resigned the office of Alderman and as having been thanked by the Mayor's Court on 20th December 1763 for his long services in that capacity to the Court.

Nowroji Road. *(From Thomas Street to Gun Carriage Street.)*

Named after Nowroji, the father of the late Edalji Machliwalla, who owned property in the village of Colaba. There is a well in the locality inscribed: "This well was constructed at the cost of Edulji Nowroji Bhicajee for the use of the public and animals, 6th February 1851."

Oak Lane. *(From Medows Street to Esplanade Road.)*
(*See* Ash Lane.)

Old Bengalpura Street. *(From Carnac Road to Janjikar Street.)*

Old Hanuman Lane. *(From Kalbadevi Road to Princess Street.)*

Old Nagpada Road. *(From Nishanpada Road to Memonwada Road.)*

Old Purbhadevi Road. *(From Portuguese Church Street to Worli Sluice.)*

Old Woman's Island.

Campbell's *Materials* etc., Ill, p. 667, has the following: "From very shortly after the establishment of British power in Bombay till the close of the eighteenth century the common name for Lower Colaba that is for the part of Colaba nearest Bombay, was Old Woman's Island. The earliest reference that has been traced is Fryer's who in 1673 (*New Account*, 67) mentions the great Malabar point abutting against Old Woman's Island. A rudely carved red-smeared goddess, a venerable Portuguese dame, a wrinkled fate-reading fisherwoman, an antique mother of harlots have all been invented to explain the name Old Woman's Island. The Portuguese seem to have known the island by no other name than Koluan, the Koli hamlet. This, by the dropping of the initial K, Dr. Gerson Da Cunha thinks the British sailor twisted into Oluan or Old Woman. In 1750 Grose (*Voyage*, I. 58) notices that the origin of the name Old Woman is unknown. A report on the fisher people of Bombay in 1747 (*Materials*, II, 147) contrasts the rates paid by the Kolis of Moory (Mori) in Warli and by the Woomanys. This, though evidently a reference to the Kolis of Colaba, can hardly be a corruption of Old Woomanys. It suggests the Hindustani Omani, the common Persian and Arab name (compare Brigg's

Ferishta, I, 413) for the sea that washes Western India. It seems possible that as the fishers have their stakes in the open sea, the Colaba Kolis were known as Al Omanis, the deep-sea fishers. It is somewhat against this explanation that no memory of the use of such a name remains.

Ollivant Bridge.

Named after Sir Edward Charles Kayll Ollivant, I.C.S., born 1846. Municipal Commissioner, Bombay, 1881-90. Member of Council, Bombay, 1897-1902.

Ormiston Road. (*Colaba Causeway near Tramway Company's Offices.*)

Named after the brothers Ormiston, Civil Engineers. Thomas Ormiston (died 1882), the elder brother, was Chief Engineer of the Port Trust from its formation in June 1873 to June 1882. He planned and constructed the Prince's Dock, Prong's Lighthouse, etc. A statue of him was erected in the University Gardens in 1888. George Ormiston (1844-1913) was Chief Engineer of the Port Trust from July 1882 to May 1892.

Outram Road. (*From Waudby Road to Hornby Road.*)

Named after General Outram (1803-1863), the famous "Bayard of India". His great rival, Charles Napier, is commemorated by a road close by. Outram was in the Bombay Army.

Ovalwadi. (*A blind lane from Vithalwadi.*)

Named after the Wovali or Bakul trees existing in the locality. Brandis (*Indian Trees,* p. 425) identifies this tree as Mimusops Elengi, known as *Owli or Wovali* in Marathi, and as *Bakul* in Kanarese. It is a large, evergreen tree, common in the west of India. The large white flowers are very fragrant and garlands of them are worn by Hindu women in their hair.

Owen Dunn Road. (*Improvement Trust Scheme IV, Road, 1911.*)

Because of the connection which G. Owen Dunn (Chairman of

the Improvement Trust, 1904—1909) had with the development of this estate. Mr. Owen Dunn (born 1854) was in the P. W. D. from 1876 till his retirement in 1909. He was President of the Corporation, 1908-09.

Paidhownie Road. *(From Parel Road to Dongri Street.)*

"Before the sea was excluded by reclamation works it used to pour across what is now called the Byculla Flats and invaded nearly the whole of Khetwadi. Its water swept through Duncan Road onwards through the Bhendi Bazaar to the spot where a slight elevation occurs upon the road, in the vicinity of the great metal market of the Presidency and where a heavy carriages roll announces the hollow beneath, at the site near where the temple of Mumbadevi now stands and is known as Payadhoni, or feet washing place. It was so called because at this identical spot a small stream of salt water was left by the receding tide where on entering Bombay travelers and cattle washed their feet." (da Cunha, p. 334.)

Pakmodia Street. *(Grant Road to Guzer Street.)*

Formerly known as Shaikh Abdul Pakmodia Street.

Palki Gully. *(From Mahim Bazaar Road to Lady Jamsetji Road.)*

Palki Street. *(Near Kambekar Street, Bhendi Bazaar.)*

So called because palanquins, used by Khojas at the time of their marriages, were kept here for hire. Among Khojas, the bride and bridegroom sit in a palanquin which forms part of the marriage procession. Palkis were until recent years used in particular by doctors.

Paltan Road. *(From Carnac Road to Hornby Road.)*

Paltan, a regiment. Named after the native infantry lines formerly situated along this road.

Panchayat Wadi. *(A blind lane from Bhuleshwar Street.)*

Panchayat (Hindi, from panch, five.) "A committee or court of arbitration consisting of five persons. But the term is widely used irrespective of the number of persons, and may include all the elders of a caste assembled in council, or the two or three bystanders called by a policeman to witness a search." (Whitworth's *Anglo-Indian Dictionary*.)

Several Hindu castes have their meeting places in this Wadi. Hence the name.

Panday Road. *(From Cuffe Parade to Wodehouse Road.)*
Named after the founder of the Parsi Sanitarium—the late Mr. Merwanji Framji Panday (1812-1876)—on the south of this road. He was the brother-in-law of the first Sir Dinshah Petit and a large mill-owner. The Trustees of the Sanitarium contributed Rs. 18,500 towards the construction of the road.

Panjrapol Road. *(From Bhuleshwar Street to Parel Road.)*
Panjrapol *(Gujarati, from panjra, Sanskrit pinjara - cage, and pol, an enclosed yard)*

"A hospital where broken down, maimed or useless animals are kept alive." (Whitworth's

Anglo-Indian Dictionary.) The panjrapol from which the road derives its name was founded, probably by leading Hindu and Parsi merchants, prominent among whom were Motichand Amichand (1783-1836) and the first Sir Jamsetji, on the 18th October 1834, and is situated near the Cowasji Patel Tank, in close proximity to the Madhav Baug. A full account of it is given in the *Bombay City Gazetteer*, Vol. Ill, p. 316.

Panton Bunder.
Named after Mr. Arthur Panton, a former Traffic Manager of the Port Trust Bunders, who entered the service of the Trust in 1876.

Paper Mill Lane. *(A blind lane from Girgaum Road.)*
Named after the paper mill that existed here.

Parel Road. *(From Kalbadevi Road to Kalachauki Road.)*

"According to a statement at page 50 of the Monthly Miscellany for 1850, Parel is a shortened form of non-pareil, the Peerless. This joke may possibly have been suggested by Neibuhr's French remark, 1763-64, *Voyage* II., 12, that in the whole of India there is nothing equal 'point de Pareille' to Parel's splendid dining and ballrooms. . . . There seems no reason to doubt that the name of the house is taken from the name of the village. The probable origin of the village name is the tree pared or padel Heterophragma chelonoides, or Bignonia suaveolens, the Tree Trumpet Flower." (Campbell, m:-695.)

Mr. S. M. Edwardes says (*Gazetteer*, I, 28) that "it is equally likely that the name is a shortened form of Parali, given by the Panchkalshi community to commemorate the shrine of Vaijanath Mahadeo at Parali in the Deccan."

Part of the road, from Paidhoni to Grant Road, is known as Bhendy Bazar. "From its row of *bhendis*, Hibiscus populnea, north of Paidhoni." (Campbell, III., 595.) According to Sir G. Birdwood, the Bhendy tree is *Thespesia populnea*, in Southern India commonly called Portia, a favourite ornamental tree, thriving best near the sea. In Ceylon, it is called Suria gansuri and also the Tulip tree. (*Hobson-Jobson.*)

Parel Government Gate Road. *(From the junction of Suparibaug and Parel Chawl Roads to South Gate of Government House meeting Parel Back Road.)*

This name, of which the origin is obvious, is commonly shortened into Government Gate Road.

Parsi Bazaar Street.[55] *(From Elphinstone Circle to Gunbow Street.)*

It was occupied by Parsi shopkeepers.

Parsi Panchayat Lane. *(From Parsi Bazaar Street to a house.)*

The offices of the Parsi Panchayat (see under Panchayat) are situated here.

Patakwadi Road. *(Improvement Trust Scheme II, Road 5, 1911.)*

Patak, or more correctly Pathak, is the surname of one of the old families of Bombay priests. There was another Pathakwadi in Girgaum which was until lately known as Baba Pathak Wadi. Baba Pathak was a great Sanskrit scholar, the author of the Sanskrit work Sanskar Bhaskar, who was often consulted by European scholars.

Pathan Street. *(From Falkland Road to Durgadevi Road.)*

Named after Pathans who live in this locality.

Pawai Road. *(A blind road from Mount Pleasant Road.)*

Named after the village of Pawai, in Thana District, on account of the owner of that village, Framji Cowasji Bomanji (1767-1837), a well known Parsi, formerly owning large properties along this road.

Pedder Road.[56] *(From Warden Road to Gowalia Tank Road).*

Named after Mr. W. G. Pedder, Municipal Commissioner (1879). He was in the Bombay Civil Service, 1855-1879, and on his retirement was appointed Secretary to the Revenue and Commerce Department at the India Office.

Peerkhan Lane. *(From Bellasis Road to New Nagpada Road.)*

So called from a Mahomedan resident named Peer Khan, a well-known stone mason.

Pestonji Street. *(From Gun Carriage Street to Shroff Street.)*

A house in the locality was owned in 1845 by Pestonji Edulji

Shroff. It passed in 1872 to (? his son) Edulji Pestonji Shroff. The street apparently is named after one or other of these two. (*See also* Shroff Street.)

Picket Road. *(From Carnac Road to Kalbadevi Road.)*
So named from a military picket house having been situated at the south end of the Road.

Pilot Bunder Road. *(Touching Colaba Road near St. John the Evangelist Church.)*
Named after the Bunder of the same name. A lifeboat was once kept here. (*Bombay City Gazetteer*, I., 55.)

Pimpalwadi Cross Lane. *(A blind lane from Mugbhat.)*
This is called Pimpalwadi on account of the many *pipal* (*Ficus Religiosa*, or the Peepul) trees that existed there. There are still one or two large peepul trees in this oart.

Pinjari Street. *(From Abdul Rehman Street to Sarang Street.)*
*Pinjari*s, cotton cleaners, live in the locality. The *pinjar* is the harp-shaped bow carrying the string by the vibration of which the cotton is cleaned or scutched. (*Vide* Tribes and Castes of the C. P., Vol. II., p. 72.)

Piru Lane. *(From Parel Road to Imamwada.)*
Named after a Havaldar of a Governor whose name was Piru.

Pitha Street. *(From Gunbow Street to Ghoga Street.)*
Named after an old *pitha* or liquor shop that exists here. It belonged to Baja Lalchu, a well known Parsi.

Platform Road. *(On both sides of Tardeo siding.)*
A matter-of-fact railway name.

Police Court Lane. *(From Bora Bazar Street to Raghunath Dadaji Street.)*
The old Fort Police Court building was at the corner of Hornby Road and Raghunath Dadaji Street, at the west end of this lane.

This old Police Court Building was the property of the first Sir Jamsetji (1783-1859) who gave it to his third son Sorabji (1825-1883) and from him, it passed to the Sassons.

Poona Street. *(From Clive Road to Frere Road.)*
Named after the town of Poona.

Popatwadi, or 1st Kolbhat Lane. *(A blind lane from Kalbadevi Road.)*
Formerly known as Moroba Popatji's wadi. Moroba Popatji was a wealthy Pathare Kshatriya of Bombay.

Portuguese Church Street, *(From Dadar and Lady Jamsetji Road junction to Old Purbhadevi Road.)*
The Rev. Father Hull writes: "This Street is so called because of Salvacao Church which still exists along with it, opposite the big tank which is called the Church tank. Salvacao church (Nossa Senhora do Salvacao) was built by the Portuguese Franciscans sometime before 1600 (said to be 1596). It has been rebuilt several times and retains nothing of its original form and appearance. It was successively in the hands of the Franciscans and the Carmelites, and passed backward and forwards between the two jurisdictions; but since 1853 has been in possession of the Padroado clergy".

St. Michael's, Mahim, near the bridge to Bandra, has a similar history; it is said to have been founded in 1534. The chapel of St. Teresa, Girgaum, often called the Portuguese chapel, was originally built in 1773; always under Propaganda Jurisdiction.

"The native Christians (and their churches) owe their name Portuguese to their having originally been converted by the Portuguese before the English acquisition. The name stuck to them till very recent times. Properly only those Christians should be called Portuguese who come from Goa (the Goans). The Padroado churches can be called Portuguese in the sense that they are under a Portuguese Bishop and manned by Goan clergy."

On the subject of Portuguese relics in Bombay, which one might expect to be commemorated in place names, Father Hull writes: "It is claimed that some old walls in the castle represent the remnants of the Portuguese Governor's house; but this is not at all certain, in fact quite improbable. The Portuguese (1534-1661) did not take Bombay island very seriously. They merely divided the land among some of the better families, and there were never more than 14 such families on the island. They built nothing known to us except just the Governor's house above alluded to, which was probably a poor affair. They made no forts either. Whether those little round towers on hills were built by them I cannot say, but probably not. The churches of Esperanca, Gloria, Salvacao, and St. Michael's and the shell of the church at Parel (now embodied in the laboratory) are the only known Portuguese buildings; and of these no distinguishing original feature survives, as they were much rebuilt. Alleged Portuguese houses; etc are mythological. With churches should be included crosses of the Portuguese type, but it is not certain which of them were made in Portuguese times and which later."

Prescott Road. *(From Napier Road to Outram Road.)*
Named after Miss Prescott. "The Frere-Fletcher school was formerly known as Miss Prescott's Fort Christian School. This building, like the University Hall and Library, dates its origin from the share mania times. Its existence is the result of the unselfish labours of Miss Prescott, a lady who for some years devoted her life and her means to the education of a few children irrespective of caste or creed. Some friends on her behalf appealed to Sir Bartle Frere, who made a grant of the land, on which the building stands, free of cost. Mr. Premchund Roychund likewise assisted by a gift of money, but the greater part of the expense has been borne by Miss Prescott, who collected the necessary funds from friends and others interested in a good cause. The foundations were laid in 1871." (Maclean's *Guide to Bombay*, p. 231.)

Prince's Dock.

The foundation stone of this dock was laid by the Prince of Wales (afterward King Edward VII) in 1875.

Princess Street. *(From Sheik Memon Street to Queen's Road.)*

The first important street scheme was undertaken by the Bombay Improvement Trust. Acquisition of property commenced September 1901; street opened and named by T.R.H. The Prince and Princess of Wales, November 10th, 1905. (Details of the scheme were prepared, in pamphlet form, by the Trust for the opening ceremony.)

Procter Road. *(From Grant Road Bridge to Girgaum Back Road.)*

Named after Sir H. E. Procter, of the firm of Killick Nixon & Co. He was born in 1866 and first came to Bombay in 1888 in Messrs. Killick Nixon & Co. He was Chairman of the Bombay Chamber of Commerce for several years and represented it in the Bombay Legislative Council. Along this road are congregated several missionary institutions in which Sir Henry takes great interest. The name of the road is therefore appropriate.

The road was formerly called Dhanji Street from a Parsi Dhanjibhai Framji but it was altered to the present name by the Municipality.

Queen's Road.[57] *(From Churchgate Street to New Queen's Road.)*

Named after Queen Victoria.

Queen's Road Bandstand. *(From Churchgate Street to Wodehouse Bridge, East approach)*

The bandstand is situated at the junction of this road with Mayo road. Formerly known as Queen's Parade, and then as Queen's road.

Fashion has somewhat deserted the Bandstand since the

mid-nineteenth century when Buist wrote: "The Bandstand on the Esplanade is the principal place of resort on weekdays; on Sundays, the Breach is the place of rendezvous."

Raghoonath Dadaji Street. *(From Hornby Road to Gunbow Street.)*

Named after Raghunath Dadaji, a rich Hindu merchant, whose family had a well-known house there. His more famous brother was Dhakji Dadaji (1760-1846) who built, in 1831, Mahaluxmi temple with its imposing pagoda.

"The one vestige of a Prabhu settlement in the Fort is Raghunath Dadaji Street." (K. N. Kabraji quoted in *Bombay City Gazetteer*, I., 242.)

Raichor Street. *(From Clive Road to Frere Road.)*

Named after Raichur in the Madras Presidency.

Rampart Row.[58] *(From Esplanade Road to Apollo Street.)*

Rampart Row West was formerly called Rope Walk Street, "so called from the Rope Walk here kept for many years by the Company for the manufacture of coir ropes." (Maclean's *Guide to Bombay*.) "Here is also a rope walk, which for length, situation, and convenience, equals any in England, that in the king's yard at Portsmouth only excepted; and like that, it has a covering to protect the workmen; cables, and all sorts of lesser cordage, both of hemp and coir, are manufactured here." (Milburn's *Oriental Commerce*—published 1825, p. 123.)

Michael (*History of the Municipal Corporation*, p. 408) writes that "Rampart Road East, or the Eastern Boulevard", was opened in 1868. Rampart Road East was subsequently renamed as part of Esplanade Road.

Rauli Hill.

Ravelin Street. (From Hornby Road to Waudby Road.)

Named after a ravelin of the old fort. (Ravelin—an outwork of two faces forming a salient angle outside the main ditch before the curtain.) The various ravelins must have often been used as landmarks. An advertisement in the *Bombay Courier* of 1828 mentions a house near the "Southwest ravelin near the Apollo Gate".

Reay Road. *(From DeLima Street to Kalachauki Road.)*
Named after Lord Reay (born 1830), Governor of Bombay from 1885-1890. The road was handed over to the Municipality by the Port Trust, 1894-5.

Rebsch Street. *(From Club Back Road to Gell Street.)*
After Mr. S. Rebsch (born 1853), Chairman of the Improvement Trust (1900-1906). He was in the Public Works Department from 1875 to 1906.

Reynolds Road. *(From Club Back Road to Morland Road.)*
Named after the first Engineer of the City Improvement Trust, Mr. Playford Reynolds (born 1843), of the Public Works Department.

Ridge Road.[59] *(From Gibbs Road to Walkeshwar Road.)*
It is on the Ridge of Malabar Hill.

Ripon Road. *(From Bellasis Road to Jacob's Circle.)*
Named after the Marquis of Ripon, Governor-General of India from 1880-1884. This road was built in 1885.

Roberts Road.
This road runs from Colaba Road at the southern end of the Parade ground towards Back Bay and then extends up to the gate of the old Lunatic Asylum. Although properly named Beach Road, it was generally called Asylum Road and, as there was no reason for maintaining the memory of the Lunatic Asylum (now moved to Poona); the Military Authorities desired that the road should be named Roberts Road, after the late Field Marshal Lord Roberts. This change was made in 1915.

Ropewalk Street. *(From Military Square Lane to Rampart Row.)*
(*Vide* Rampart Row.)

Rose Cottage Lane. *(From Mount Road to Matarpakhadi.)*
From a bungalow of this name.

Rotten Row Ride.
This name, borrowed from London, was applied to the ride around what is now called the Oval, but it is now seldom used. "Numerous gardens or planted enclosures have been laid out at suitable spots, such as the Rotten Row Ride, by the late Mr. Bellasis." (Maclean's *Guide to Bombay*, p. 210.)

In a letter to *The Times of India* (5th December, 1914) on a new ride laid out inside the Race Course, an anonymous writer says: "It is hardly too much to prophesy that the Rotten Row of Bombay in the future will not be the Kennedy Sea Face but the Club (Western India Turf Club) track at Mahaluxmi."

Russell Street. *(From Olive Road to 1st Clive Cross Lane.)*

Rutherfield Street. *(From Military Square Lane to Forbes Street.)*

Ryan Grain Market.
Named after Mr. John Ryan, the first Traffic Manager of the Bombay Port Trust.

Sadashiv Street. *(From Girgaum Bach Road to Kandewadi Lane.)*
Named after an owner of property there named Sadashiv, a Hindu of the Pathare Prabhu caste. The old name of this street, still current among the inhabitants, is *Raishum Gully*— *raishum* silk, *gully* lane—because silk weavers lived there and some of them are still to be found there.

Safarabadi Street. *(West of Morland Road.)*
So named because the inhabitants were mostly engaged on ships. *Safar* means a voyage. The Street is called Mahomedan Street by the Municipality.

Samuel Road. *(From Sandhurst Road to Bhandari Street.)*
Samuel Street was formerly known as Shamji (or Samaji) Hassaji Street. It was named after Shamji Husaji who was a commandant in the native army of the Bombay Government in 1790. In commemoration of his escape from the hands of Hyder Ali of Mysore, he built the synagogue known as the Gate of Mercy. Many other houses in the locality were owned by and occupied by Bene Israels. The street is named after him (Shamji) because Shamji is synonymous with Samuel. Essajee Hasaji, the brother of Shamji, was an officer in the native army at the same time as his brother. The street now called Bardan Street was formerly known as Essajee Hasaji Street. (See *Bombay City Gazetteer*, Vol. I., p. 249.)

Sandhurst Road.[60] *(From Frere Road to Girgaum Road.)*
Named after Lord Sandhurst, Governor of Bombay (1895-1900). It was in his governorship that the Act was passed which constituted the City Improvement Trust which built this road. The road was handed over to the Municipality in 1910.

Sankli Street. *(From Morland Road to Clare Road.)*
Named after a tank of this name that formerly existed here. It was called Sanklia, or Sakaria because its water was considered to be as sweet as "sakar" (sugar candy). Another and equally plausible explanation is that the tank got its name from being surrounded by *sankel*, or iron chain railings, instead of a stone parapet. The tank was rilled up in 1893, and the site of it is now occupied by a fire-brigade station and Municipal ward offices.

Sarang Street. *(From Carnac Road to Bhajipala Street.)*
Formerly known as Baloo Sarang Street. Sarang means "boatswain": the word is Persian—*sarhang*—and originally meant a commander or overseer. In modern Persian, it seems to be used for a colonel. (*Hobson-Jobson.*)

Church Gate

Oval Maidan

Sassoon Dock.

"The Sassoon Dock at Colaba is situated close to the present Cotton Green and was opened in 1875 by Messrs. D. Sassoon & Co. In 1879 it was purchased by Government on behalf of the Port Trustees." (*Bombay City Gazetteer*, Vol. III., p. 264.)

Sayad Mukri Street. *(From Bhandari Street to Dongri Street.)*

Believed to be named after Mahomed Sayad Mukri. In Arabic, *mukri* means one which reads certain passages from the Koran in the course of a sermon.

Scandal Point. *(Breach Candy.)*

The name is to be found in the Monthly Miscellany of Western India (1850) if not earlier. The explanation is obvious, for the popularity of drives to this point has not diminished. "There are two drives especial favourites with the Bombay fashionable world: one to the Esplanade, the other to the 'Breach' on the western side of the island." (Lady Falkland *Chow-Chow*, Vol. I, p. 97.)

"On Sundays, the Breach is the place of rendezvous, though the churches commonly draw the bulk of the fashionables away." (Buist's *Guide*, p. 274 b.)

Scottish Orphanage Gully. *(From Lady Jamsetji Road to Mahim Bazar Road.)*

Named after the well-known school in Mahim.

Setalwad Road. *(From Nepean Sea Road seawards.)*

Named after C. H. Setalwad, a member of the Bombay Corporation, who has his bungalow there.

Sewri Road. *(From Kalachowki Road to Sewri Koliwada and crossroad junction.)*

"Sivri, or Sewri, which Fryer referred to as Suri, is held to derive its name from Sivadi or Sivavadi (the place or garden of Siva) or possibly from Shivarvadi." (*Bombay City Gazetteer*, Vol. I., p.

30). As a place name, Sewri is most commonly applied to the Christian cemetery, but it occurs also in three or four street names.

Shaik Budan Comodin Street. (*From Grant Road to Bellasis Road.*)

The municipal spelling of the name is peculiar, but the street appears to derive its name from a prominent resident of former days, Shaikh Buran Kammudin, a Konkani Mahomedan. It is now known among the residents as Teli Moholla or Teli Street. *Teli*—oilmen, of whom some live in this street.

Shamsett Street. (*From Abdul Rehman Street to Sheik Memon Street.*)

Named after Balaji Shamsett, a wealthy Hindu of the Sonar or goldsmith caste, related to the famous Jagonnath Sunkersett (1802-1865). He had several houses in the Street which were formerly inhabited exclusively by Hindu tailors, which was called from this circumstance Chhipichali, i.e., a lane of tailors.

Sheik Memon Street. (*From Carnac Road, Crawford Market to Kalbadevi Road.*)

This is named after a Deccani Mahomedan Pir, or holy man, called Shaikh Momin, corrupted into Memon, who flourished 150 years ago. The Saint's tomb or Darga is in this street near its junction with Princess Street and is frequented by many Mahomedans who make offerings there. An Annual religious fair is also held on the anniversary of the Saint's death.

A lawsuit—"Mahomed Husan Aswari and others versus Gulam Mohidin Baig and others"—was reported in *The Times of India* on December 1, 1914. The plaintiffs applied for the appointment of a receiver of the valuable properties attached to the Dargah of Sheikh Momin, from which the well-known Sheikh Memon Street takes its name. They contend that the properties were charitable and must be declared to have been held by the defendants as matavalis or managers of the Dargah, and the defendants should be made to account for the rents of shops, over Rs. 250 a month; for the Rs. 20,000 or so they had received as compensation for set-back from the Municipality; for offerings at the shrine or tomb of the Pir Sheikh Momin; and for other receipts. The charity was founded about one-and-a-half centuries ago. Counsel for the defendants denied that the properties mentioned were either public or charitable contrariwise, they were proprietary and ancestral, for which the defendants paid income-tax and municipal and other dues. The defendants were the descendants of the relatives of the Sheikh Momin; there was at the same place the tomb of Kahimuddin Shah also, an ancestor of theirs. The tombs of the two Pirs or saints were situated in the family house of the defendants which had recently been rebuilt. The notice of motion was dismissed. Sections of the street are known to natives as Kapad-bazaar or cloth market; Chandi or Shroff bazaar, silver market; Moti or Javeri bazaar, pearl market; cloth, silver, and pearl-merchants having their establishments in this locality.

Shekadi Lane. *(A blind lane from Viihalwadi.)*
Named after a Hindu of the Parbhu caste called Shekadi. There was a well in the middle of the lane now filled up which was called Shekadi's well.

Shepherd Road. (From Parel Road to Clare Road.)
Named after the Alms House of that name situated in this road.

"St. Peter's, Mazagon, was opened for Divine Service in 1859. It was built chiefly from funds bequeathed by an aged European resident of the district, named Shepherd, about whose life those who knew him best observed an air of mystery. The outside world only heard of his existence. On his death, the public learned that he had left funds for the erection of a church at Mazagon and of a refuge for widows, orphans, and blind persons. The latter, known as 'Shepherd's Alms-House', has been built at Byculla in convenient proximity to the Byculla Church". (Maclean's *Guide to Bombay*, p. 298.)

A manuscript note on the Shepherd's Trust file states that Shepherd joined the East India Company's Marine in 1787, retired in 1834 on a pension of Rs. 87-8, and died ten years later. He left Rs. 9,794 to build alms-houses.

Sholapur Street. *(From Clive Road to Frere Road.)*
Named after the City of Sholapur in the Deccan.

Shroff Street. *(From Pestonji Street to Bora and Hamal Streets.)*
Possibly named after the Pestonji Edulji Shroff who also gave his name to Pestonji Street (q.v.). It was in this quarter of the town, and especially in Bazaar Gate Street, that the Hindu Shroffs first established themselves. "Shroff—A money changer, a banker. Ar. *sarraf, sairafi, sairqf.*" (*Hobson-Jobson.*)

Sindhi Lane. *(From Falkland Road to Khetwadi Main Road.)*
People from Sind (Sindhis) live in this lane.

Sion.
"Sion, which was called Siam by Fryer and Svya by Simao Botelho (1554), is a Portuguese corruption of the Marathi Simwa, a boundary or limit, Sion village being the boundary between the island of Bombay and Salsette." (*Bombay City Gazetteer*, Vol. I., p. 29.) -Da Cunha's note on this word (*The Origin of Bombay*, p. 59) is rather confusing. He writes: "The village of Sion, which the early Portuguese more approximately to its origin wrote Siva, has some temples of its own. . . .The name Sion is derived from the Marathi Simva, a boundary or a limit, the village of Sion being the boundary between the island of Bombay and Salsette." This supposed connection with Siva may be traced farther back, for Moor in *Oriental Fragments* published in 1834 (p. 436) gives the following derivation: "Siva is, in the southern, western, and, perhaps, other parts of India, corruptly pronounced Sheo, and otherways Seo, Seu and Siv. A conical hill, among the highest, on Bombay, and the most northern is (almost of course) named

after this elevated family. Natives generally call it Seo or Sheo. It used to command the passage between Bombay and Salsette and served as a check on the Mahrattas of the latter island. We always write it Sion, and pronounce it as we do the name of our 'holy hill'. It was probably so called by our predecessors."

Sion Causeway was formerly known as Sion Vellard *(cf. Hornby Vellard.)*

Maria Graham (1812) writes (p. 8): "At the foot of the hill of Sion is a causeway or vellard which was built by Mr. Duncan, the present Governor, across a small arm of the sea, which separates Bombay and Salsette. It is well constructed of stone and has a draw-bridge in the middle, but it is too narrow for carriages to go along with safety in bad weather; however, it is of great advantage to the farmers and gardeners who bring in the daily supplies of provisions to the Bombay market. The vellard was begun in A.D.1797, and finished in 1805, at the expense of 50,575 rupees, as I learned from an inscription over a small house at the end next Bombay, where a guard is kept to prevent the introduction of contraband articles from Salsette, which though under the English government, is still subject to the Mahratta regulations with regard to taxes."

Siri Road. *(From Walkeshwar Road to Ridge Road.)*

"This road is called Siri from the Marathi word *sidi,* a ladder or a staircase, from its steep or slanting position on the way from Chaupati to Malabar Hill." (da Cunha, p. 56.)

Sleater Road. *(From Falkland Road to Grant Road. From Tardeo Road to the Low-Level Road south of Falkland Bridge.)*

The road was made on the land of which part belonged to the B. B. & C. I. Railway. It is named after J. M. Sleater for many years Resident Engineer of the B.B.&.C.I. Railway and Chief Engineer, 1882-1892.

Sonapur Street. *(From Girgaum Road to Chandanwadi Lane.)*

Named according to one explanation after the Hindu Burial Ground close by; and called Sonapur from the vernacular meaning sleeping place, or a quarter of the town. *Sona* means sleep.

Rao Bahadur P. B. Joshi writes: "I don't think this is correct. *Sone* in Marathi means gold and *pur* a city. Hindus call a cemetery a *Smashan* or *Shamshanpur*, and this *Smashanpur* was probably changed into Suvashpur or Sonapur, that is, the city of gold. When an aged person dies it is a common practice to say '*tyachen sone jhalen*', i.e., he is turned into gold. Another explanation for the origin of the name is that this, or an adjoining wadi or oart, was known by the name of Sonawadi and so the new burning ground was named after the wadi."

Sorabji Suntook Lane. *(From Lohar Street to Wellington Street.)*

(*See* Dady Santook Lane.)

Souter Street. *(From Gilder Street to Morland Road.)*

Named after a former Police Commissioner, Sir Frank Henry Souter, Kt. C.S.I. (1832-88). He was the son of Captain Souter, who was a prisoner in Afghanistan in 1842 in the hands of the notorious Akbar Khan. He took part in suppressing dacoity in Southern Deccan consequent on the Mutiny of 1857. Commissioner of Police, Bombay, in succession to Forjett, from 1864 till his death in 1888. He was knighted by King Edward when he visited Bombay in 1875, as Prince of Wales. He took a prominent part in Municipal affairs and was twice (1882 and 1883) President of the Municipal Corporation, as well as of the Town Council.

St. George's Road. *(From the south-east gate of the Victoria Terminus to Frere Road.)*

Named after the European General Hospital of the same name.

Stable Street *(From Bapty Road to 13th Kamatipura Street.)*

Named after the Municipal Health Department stables situated there.

Stevens Street. *(From Apollo Pier Road to Lansdowne Road.)*

The Yacht Club Chambers, the only building in this street, was built under the supervision of the late Mr. F. W. Stevens but was designed by Mr. J. Adams, the Government Architect. They were opened in 1898.

Store Lane. *(From Homji Street to Parsee Bazar Street.[61])*

Named after the commissariat stores close by.

Strand Road. *(Prom Apollo Pier to Henry Road.)*

Named so because it is situated abutting the Harbour wall.

Subedar Lane or Cowasji Subedar Lane. *(East of Patil Street but no longer exists.)*

Named after Cowasji Limji Subedar, a well known Parsi of the latter part of the eighteenth century. He was a Subedar or Inspector in the Customs Department and had a house in this street. His dates are not certain but his son Shapurji Cowasji Subedar (1770-1823) who succeeded to his father's place in the Customs, died in 1823, aged 53. This lane is mentioned with others in the official report of the great fire of 1803 given in *Historical Materials*, Part I., p. 433. (*Bombay Gazetteer*, Vol. XXVI., pt. I.)

Suklaji Street. *(From Bellasis Road to Grant Road.)*

So named after Kharshedji Jamasji Banatwala (1809-1870) who owned a large property in the locality. Sukhlaji was Kharshedji's uncle and he and his brother Jamasji (Kharshedji's father) traded in sackcloth (hence their surname Banatwala, *"banat"* meaning sack-cloth) under the name Sukhlaji and Jamasji. This trade name became famous among Parsis, and Kharshedji was known by this name Sukhlaji-Jamasji, shortened into Sukhlaji, rather than by his surname.

Suleman Street. *(West Agripada.)* 1911.
Mr. Haji Suleman Abdul Wahed, Sheriff of Bombay, 1910, owns property in this street which is called after him.

Sunder Lane. *(A blind lane from Haines Road.)*
So named after Soonder Bai, a Hindu woman, well known formerly in the locality, who had a house in the lane. It is also known as Chickal Gully, or Mud Lane, because before the district was drained, rain water used to accumulate here and there was much mud. There is Chickal Gully or Wadi near Sleater Road, Grant Road, called by the inhabitants from the same cause "the district of mud" or chickal.

Supari Baug Road. *(From Parel Road to Dadar and Naigaum Cross Roads.)*
Named after a plantation or garden (Persian, bagh) of *supari* this is the best known vernacular name for the betelnut palm *(areca catechu)*.

Surat Street. *(From Musjid Station Road to Frere Road.)*
Named after the City of Surat.

Surati Street. *(East of Duncan Road, near Mastan Tank.)*
So called from Surati Dhed or scavengers from Surat who reside there. There was in this street a tank, now filled up, called from its dirty state Gunda Talao, *gunda* dirty.

Sussex Road. *(From Connaught Road to Parel Road.)*

Sutar Chawl Street. *(From Abdul Rehman Street to Shaik Memon Street.)*
So named from houses of "Sutaras" or carpenters there. Sutar (Hindi form of *sutardhar*). The name of a Sudra caste; they are carpenters. They are looked upon as of intermediate Sudra rank in most places, but in some, as Midnapur, they are held to be a low caste. (Whitworth's *Anglo-Indian Dictionary*.)

Sydenham Road. *(To be constructed from Crawford Market to Sandhurst Road.)*

Extract from the proceedings of a meeting of the Bombay Improvement Trust held on the 4th March 1913: "Considered papers underlying Circular No. 91 of 1913 on the following minute by the Chairman, dated 22nd February 1913, suggesting that the main road in the Sandhurst Road to Crawford Market Street Scheme is named 'Sydenham Road'.

I suggest that the Board should, in recognition of the strong support which Lord Sydenham had always given to them during his term of office as Governor of Bombay, ask him, before he leaves Bombay, to kindly consent to their giving the name Sydenham Road to the new road to be constructed between Crawford Market and Sandhurst Road in Scheme 37. It will be some years before the new road can be actually constructed; but it will be convenient to have a name for it at once, so that the Scheme may be known as the Sydenham Road Scheme instead of the Sandhurst Road to Crawford Market Street Scheme.

The Chairman has proposed the adoption of the suggestion Mr. Wacha proposed as an amendment that the new road is named 'New Memonwada Road'. The amendment being put to the vote was lost. The original proposition being put to the vote was carried. Mr. Wacha alone dissenting. The Chairman's suggestion was adopted."

Sir George Sydenham Clarke, 1st Baron Sydenham of Combe (born 1848) was Governor of Bombay 1907-1913.

Tad-Wadi *(From Girgaum Road to Sonapur Street.)*

Tarvadi or Tadvadi—the Brab-garden. (*Bombay City Gazetteer*, I., 27.) The palmyra palm *(Borassus flabeltiffer)* is called *tad* in Marathi. The name "brab", commonly used in Bombay, is derived from the Portuguese *brava*, "wild palm".

Tamarind Lane. *(From Medows Street to Dean Lane.)*

The tamarind after which this lane is called was a famous

tree beneath which it was customary to hold public auctions. It stood near the Cathedral at the edge of the cotton green, and was responsible for the phrase *amli-agal* "in front of the tamarind"— *amli* being Hindustani as *chinch* is Marathi for tamarind)—by which the hack-carriage drivers of earlier years denoted the Cathedral. This tree was cut down in November 1846. (See *Bombay City Gazetteer*, III., 251.) Tamarind trees were once common here, but the only survivor of importance is one at the N. E. corner of the Cathedral compound.

Tandel Street. *(From Jail Road south to 1st Chinch Bunder Road.)*

Tandel is another form of Tindal; and for this variety of street name, cf. Sarang Street. Hobson-Jobson gives the following note:

Tindal. Mai. *Tandal,* Tel, tandelu, also in Mahr and other vernacular *tandel, tandail*—The head or commander of a body of men; but in ordinary specific application a native petty officer of Lascars, whether on board ship (boatswain) or in the ordnance department, and sometimes the head of a gang of labourers on public works.

Tank Bunder Road. *(From Ghorupdeo and Mount Road Junction to Reay Road.)*

There is a large tank in the vicinity of this Bunder.

Tank Street. *(From Grant Road to Bellasis Road.)*

Khandia Tank formerly existed between this street and Khandia Tank Street.

Tankerville.

A house situated close to the site on which was the Gowalia Tank, until 1912 when it was reclaimed, and near the foot of the north-eastern slope of Malabar Hill. Hence its name, though the punning allusion to Tankerville in Normandy, whence a famous Anglo-Norman family (of the Greys) derived the title of its earldom in the fifteenth century, had much to do with it.

For the Anglo-Indian word Tank in the sense of a large sheet of water, *vide Hobson-Jobson*.

Mr. R. P. Karkaria writes: "Tankerville is a very old bungalow, and its late proprietor Mr. Hirji Readymoney (1809-1901), grandfather of the present baronet Sir Cowasji Jehangir, showed me in 1893 some old papers in which it was stated that the Gowalia Tank, as well as Tankerville, belonged to a civil servant of the Company, a member of the Bombay Council, already in 1765 or thereabouts. It belonged to the Readymoney family for more than a century. From 1854 to 1869 the Elphinstone College was housed in it; at the end of the latter year the College was removed to a building specially built for it at Byculla opposite the Victoria Gardens where it remained till 1888 in which year it was transferred to its present building opposite the new Museum, and the old one at Byculla came into the possession of the Technical Institute. At a stone's throw from Taukerville is another bungalow also called after the Gowalia Tank, Tankar Villa. It formerly had a large compound, part of which adjoined the Tank. A great part of this compound was lately built upon and forms the site of Khalakdina Terrace, so called from the name of the mother of the present owner Mr. Kasamally Jairazbhai Peerbhai. Tankar Villa was long in the possession of the Shroff family, its owner has been a brother of the well known Parsi reformer Maneckji Cursetji (1808-87)."

Tankerville is often referred to by old writers as a prominent landmark, as indeed it must have been until the vicinity was built over. For example, Buist's *Guide to Bombay* (p.171) says: "The Malabar Hill ridge is partly broken across near Tankerville, by the deep hollow through which the public road passes."

Tantantpura Street. *(From Samuel Street to Nishanpara Road.)*

Tara Naikin's Oart. *(A blind lane from Kolbhat Street.)*
Presumably named after a charmer named Tara. "*Naikan* - A dancing girl. This word is the feminine form of *naik* and so means either the wife of a *naik* or a mistress. But naik and

naikan (or the other feminine form *nayika*) are used to denote the hero and heroine—the lover and his mistress—in plays and poems, and it seems to be through this meaning of the word that naikan has come to be used euphemistically for dancing girl or courtesan." (Whitworth's *Anglo-Indian Dictionary*.)

Tardeo Road.[62] *(From Gowalia Tank Road to Clerk Road and Warden Road Junction.)*

Named after the temple of Tardeo. *Tar or tad*, palm; and *Deo, dev, or dewa*, god. *cf.* Tadwadi.

Tava Lane. *(From Abdul Rehman Street to Narayan Dhuru Street.)*

Two suggested derivations are put forward: (1) Iron dishes in which to bake bread (*tava*) are made and sold here. (2) *Tava* is also a Bora surname and, as Boras reside in this locality, that may possibly be the origin of the name.

Tejpal Road. *(Improvement Trust Scheme IV, Road 5 A., 1911.) (Adjoins the Tejpal Estate.)*

Named after Goculdas Tejpal (1822-1867), a Hindu philanthropist who founded the Hospital in Carnac Road called after him. The Tejpal Sanskrit Boarding School and the Laxmi Narayan Temple, built by the Tejpal family, are along this Road.

Telwadi. *(From Vithalwady to Vithalwady.)*

Tel in Hindi, *taila* in Sanskrit, means oil—especially gingelly or sesame oil—from *tila* the sesamum seed. There are oil shops in the lane, and there was formerly an oil press there.

Temker Street. *(From Grant Road to Bellasis Road.)*

Mr. R. P. Karkaria writes: "So called from a Temur tree which grew there in past years and which some inhabitants told me they had seen. This tree has small leaves which when dried are used for making 'biddies' or native cigarettes. The name *Temur* does not occur in the list of vernacular names in Brandis' *Indian Trees*.

Thakurdwar Road.[63] *(From Girgaum Back Road to Queen's Road.)*

Thakurdwar is a generic name that is not uncommon. It means literally the door of an idol, and so an idol-house, a temple. The Thakurdwar at Girgaum, after which this road is called, is an interesting temple, dedicated to Rama. It is known as Atmaram Bawa's Thakurdwar, after the Hindu sage of that name (died 1836, aged 90) who built it. (da Cunha, p. 63.)

Thana Street. *(From Frere Road to Clive Road.)*

Named after the town of Thana on the G.I.P. Railway near Bombay.

Theatre Road. *(From Hornby Road to Ravelin Street and Murzban Road.)*

Named after the Novelty Theatre close by.

Thomas Street. *(From Colaba Road to the East end of the Colaba Markets and from the above to the walls of the Gun Carriage factory.)*

Tod Street. *(From Parsi Bazaar Street to Hornby Road.)*

Ghoga Street, Fort, (q.v.) is known also as Tod Street from James Tod, the Lieutenant of Police, 1779-90, who had his house and chowkey here. He was for many years the first Provincial Grand Master of Freemasons in Bombay.

About this Tod, who was dismissed for corruption in 1790, see J. Mackintosh's *Minute on Police of Bombay*, apend. in Morley's Digest, 1851, Vol. II, page 513, *cf.* E. P. Karkaria in *Bombay Gazette*, 7th October 1907.

The western part of the street is also known as Bhim Street from the fact that a Parsi bone-setter named Bhimji lived here, and his descendants still practice in this street. The eastern part is commonly known as Murga Seri or Cock Lane. There is a noted well in a house there called Murga Bava's Well to which offerings are still made.

Topiwalla's Wadi Street. *(A blind lane from Girgaum Back Road eastwards.)*
Named after the owner of the Oart, Anant Shivaji Desai, Topiwalla. He has a chawl there, called Topiwalla's Chawl.

Trimbak Parshuram Street. *(From Falkland Road to Bapty Road.)*

Trinity Street. *(From Lohar Street to 1st Marine Street.)*
Named after Holy Trinity Church, of which da Cunha (*Origin of Bombay*, p. 360) gives the following account: "Holy Trinity Chapel, the gift of the Hon'ble James Farish to this City, was constructed from 1838 to 1841 by the Rev. George Candy, its first minister, ordained by Bishop Carr on Trinity Sunday, 1838, opened for divine service in 1840 and consecrated by the Rt. Rev. Daniel Wilson in 1842, at New Sonapur, to which was attached the Indo-British School for girls and boys. This Church was originally a chapel of ease to the St. Thomas' Cathedral and was subsequently raised to the status of a District Church. This building was sold about ten years ago (about 1885) and a new church and the Indo-British Institution built in a more healthy locality on the eastern part of the Esplanade (Hornby Road). The old building is now reduced to a market.

Tulloch Road. *(From Lansdowne Road to Nowroji Fardunji Road.)*
Named after Major Hector Tulloch (born 1835) formerly (1868) Executive Engineer, Bombay Municipality. He took part in constructing the Vehar Water Works and wrote a valuable work on the drainage of Bombay.

Ulster Road. *(From Parel Road to Cork Road.)*
The road was taken over from the City Improvement Trust on 1st August, 1906,—not a year of political excitement in Ireland. (*See* Connaught Road.)

Umarkhadi.

"Before the main breach was closed, all the ground from Masjid Bandar to the foot of the old Belvedere, now occupied by the Bhandarwada water reservoir, was swept by the sea running far inward. It submerged the land up to the foot of the Nowroji Hill, and within a few yards of the Umarkhadi Jail. There it formed a capacious creek resorted to by native craft. And the traditional time and circumstances are still preserved in the name of *Umar khadi*, which according to some means a mountain creek, and, according to others who derive it from *Umbhar khadi*, means the fig-tree creek." (da Cunha, p. 335.)

Undria Street. *(From Grant Road to Mustan Tank Road.)*

So called from a former Konkani Mahomedan resident named Isamuddin Baba Saheb Undre, whose family still resides there. It is also called by the inhabitants Chowky Moholla, from there being a Police Chowky in it.

University Road. *(From Esplanade Road to Mayo Road.)*

The road skirts the buildings and gardens of the Bombay University.

Vachaghandi Road. *(Improvement Trust Scheme IV, Road 6, 1911.)*

There is an Agiari of this name on the road called after Sorabji Vachaghandi (1778-1857), consecrated 8th February 1858. (*Parsi Dharmasthala*, p. 148.) The Vachaghandi family was one of the earliest Parsi families to settle in Bombay, where its heads were for several generations the Modi (grain suppliers) of the East India Company. The oldest Tower of Silence, called after them Modi's Tower of Silence, was probably built in 1672 (*cf. Bombay Bahar*, by Vacha, pp. 296-299).

Vacharaj Lane. *(Matunga.)*

Named after one Mr. Vacharaj whose family still owns a house in the lane.

Valpakhadi Road. *(From Mazagon Road to the Night Soil Depot.)*

Val, a kind of pulse or bean, *pakhadi,* a part of the town, *cf.* Mugbhat.

Vanka Moholla. *(Kalbadevi Road to Kolbhat Street.)*

Vanka, "curved". This Moholla or street has a curve in its course.

Varsova Street. *(From Kamatipura Bazaar Road to Kamatipura 15th Street and Bellasis Road.)*

Named after the village of Versova near Andheri (Salsette), the properties here being owned by the late Mr. Muljibhoy Jivraj, a Khoja merchant, who also owned an estate on the island of Mahr, opposite the sands of Versova.

Victoria Road.[64] *(From Parel Road to Reay Road.)*

Named after Queen Victoria. The Municipality took it over from the Port Trust in June 1897; the year of the Diamond Jubilee, and that event probably suggested the name.

Vincent Road. *(From Dadar Road to Sion Road.)*

Named after a former Police Commissioner, Robert W.E. Hampe Vincent. The late Mr. Vincent (1841-1914) served in the Italian Campaign of 1862 and in the following year joined His Majesty's 45th regiment in which he served until 1869 when he joined the Bombay Police. He served in Bombay City until 1883, when for six months he was Deputy Inspector-General of Police in Egypt, for which work he received from the Khedive the title of Vincent Bey. On his return to Bombay, Mr. Vincent became a D.S.P. and in April 1893 he was appointed to be Commissioner of Police, Bombay, an office which he held until January 1899. He was responsible for the erection of the existing Head Police Office opposite Crawford Market, which superseded the old Headquarters at Byculla—now occupied by the Mounted Police. (*The Times of India,* October 15th, 1914.)

Vithaldas Road. *(Improvement Trust Scheme II, Road 8, 1911.)*

Sir Vithaldas Thackersey's cloth market is on this road.

Vithalwadi. *(From Kalbadevi Road to Sheik Memon Street.)*

Named after the temple of the Hindu god Vithoba or Vithal.

Wadala Road. *(From Matunga Leper Asylum to Naigam and Sewri Cross Road Junction.)*

Da Cunha (p. 58) explains this by identifying vadali and varli which latter, he says, has three derivations. (*See below under* Worli.)

Wadi Bunder.

"*Wadi*" means in the vernacular languages, garden, and is probably so called from the Konkani Mussalmans who reside near this Bunder, as well as at Mazagon close by, having large gardens or "*wadis*" in the locality. One of these "*wadis*" must have been on the site of this bunder. (*Cf. Bombay City Gazetteer*, Vol. I, page 255, n. 4.) This bunder is the chief landing place for all kinds of country timber and other wood. (*Vide* also Wari Bunder.)

Wadia's Chawl. *(Chandanwady.)*

Named after the Parsi fire temple of this name which is in the vicinity. This fire temple, which is of the highest class, was consecrated in 1830 by the sons of Hormusji Bomanji Wadia. He was "the most prominent native citizen of Bombay during the first quarter of this (19th) century, and died on the morning of March 8, 1826, in the sixtieth year of his age. He was for more than thirty years associated with Forbes and Company. He left three sons and two daughters. He was the youngest brother of the builder Jamsetjee Bomanjee and of the celebrated merchant Pestonjee Bomanji, head of the Wadia family. The family held a strong position, and dispensed festivity at Lowji Castle from early times."

(Douglas, *Glimpses of Old Bombay*, p. 36.)

Wadia Street. *(Tardeo.)*

This street (now taken over by the Municipality) was recently constructed by the Trustees of the estate of the late (1837-1909) Mr. N.M.Wadia.

Walkeshwar Road. *(From Chaupati to Government House Upper Gate.)*

"Its name which is compounded of *Valuka* (sand) and *Ishwar* (God) and signifies the god of the sand, owes its origin to the legend that Rama when on his way to Lanka (Ceylon) in quest of Sita halted on the very spot where the Walkeshwar temple now stands. There he took the advice of certain Brahman ascetics as to what he should do in order to regain his wife from the clutches of Ravana, the demon king of Lanka, and they advised him to raise a lingam on the spot and worship Shiva or Mahadeo. Rama accordingly despatched his brother Lakshman to Benares to bring thence a lingam of supreme potency, and he himself in the meantime fashioned a lingam of the sand of the seashore and performed over it the *pranpratishta* or life creating ceremony." (*Bombay City Gazetteer*, III, 359.)

Wallace Street. *(From Hornby Road to Marxian Road.)*

The firm of Wallace and Co. was started in Bombay in the forties and moved its offices from Elphinstone Circle to its new building in this street in December 1909. It was shortly after that move that the Municipality named this newly laid out street after the firm.

Walton Road. (From Colaba Causeway to Merewether Road.)

Named after the late Mr. Rienzi G. Walton, Executive Engineer, Bombay Municipality. Vehar Lake was partly constructed under him.

Warden Road.[65] *(From Nepean Sea Road to Tardeo Road.)*

Named after Francis Warden, a prominent Bombay Civilian in the first quarter of the nineteenth century. He was Chief Secretary to Government for a long time and was in the Council from 1823-1828 when he retired and became a Director of the East India Company. He wrote a report in 1814 on the landed tenure of the City which is still valuable. This road is more than a century old.

Wari Bunder Road. *(Frere Road to Hancock Bridge. From Mazagon Road to DeLima Street.)*

Wari or *Wadi* (Marathi, from *wad*, a hedge) means an enclosure. It is the feminine form of wada and, according to Whitworth's *Anglo-Indian Dictionary*, has the following meanings: an enclosed field; a large house; a country residence of which the garden is the main feature; an enclosed hamlet distinct from the main village; a rectangle of houses with the space enclosed.

Waudby Road.[66] *(From Hornby Road to Esplanade Road.)*

A marble tablet on the wall of the Alexandra Native Girls Institution, at the south end of this road, bears the following inscription:-

"This road is named after Major Sidney James Waudby who, with Private Elahi Bux and Private Sonnak Tannak, all of the 19th Bo. Infantry fell on the 16th April 1880, in defence of the Dubrai Post in Afghanistan, which, when warned that an attack in force was imminent, they refused to abandon and most gallantly held for three hours against 300 of the enemy, many of whom were slain. Eventually, when all their ammunition was expended they dashed into the midst of their foes and died fighting. In honour of their heroism, this tablet is placed by the Regiment."

Wellington Lines. *(Known as the Cooperage.)*

The first Duke of Wellington was connected with Bombay while in India and the Bombay Government helped him much with supplies, etc., during his memorable Mahratta campaign which ended in the victory of Assaye, 1803. Bombay citizens presented him with an address when he was here in 1804 on his way home. (See Chap. 36, *Bombay and Western India* by James Douglas.)

The Wellington Fountain was erected about the year 1865 by

public subscription in memory of the Duke. "Our conscript fathers might have left us a gate by way of a souvenir (of the ramparts) instead of the nondescript things which, under the name of fountains, obstruct the highway, as if the names of Wellington and Frere were writ in water." (*Bombay and Western India*, Vol.I.p.224.) The fountain is no longer permitted to satisfy the wants of the thirsty, but it at least perpetuates the Duke's name which is more than can be said for Wellington Pier, the official designation of the Apollo Bandar. Maclean in his guide to Bombay says it was never used in common parlance, and the name would long ago have been forgotten if it were not inscribed on the Bandar wall.

Wilderness Road. *(From Ridge Road to Nepean Sea Road.)*

From a large bungalow called Wilderness situated there, where formerly some Commanders-in-Chief of the Bombay Army, like General Warre, have resided.

Malabar Hill, half a century ago, had only two bungalows built upon it—the *Beehive* and the *Wilderness*. (Maclean's *Guide to Bombay*, published in 1875, p. 309.)

"In 1840-42 Robert Wigram Crawford's bungalow was the Wilderness." (Douglas, *Glimpses of Old Bombay*, p. 20.)

Willoughby Road. *(From Marine Lines to Queen's Road.)*
Named after General Willoughby?

Winter Road. *(From Ridge Road, a blind Road.)*
Named after Mr. Winter, solicitor, of Messrs. Prescott and Winter, who had a bungalow there. The road is commonly known as "Graham Gali" because Messrs. W. A. Graham and Co. has long owned the principal house (Claremount) on it.

Wodehouse Road. *(From Esplanade to Colaba Road.)*
Named after Sir Phillip Wodehouse, Governor of Bombay 1872-1877. Born 1811, entered Ceylon Civil Service, and was

successively Superintendent of British Honduras, Governor of British Guiana, Governor of the Cape and High Commissioner in South Africa, before coming to Bombay; died 1887.

Woollen Mill Gully. *(From Lady Jamsetji Road to Tulsi Pipe Line Road.* [67]*)*

Named after the mill of this name situated in this lane.

Worli Road.[68] *(From the junction of Ferguson and Haines Roads to Cleveland Road and Worli Sluice Junction.)*

"The name Varli (Worli) has three derivations, one from the Marathi *vad,* the banian tree or *ficus indica,* on account of a forest of this tree, once abundant on that island, with the termination of *ali,* which means an alley or village. Thus, *vad* and *ali* make together a banian tree village, or *Vadali* shortened into *varli.* The second is connected with the word *var,* which means a boon or a blessing, and *varli* is said to have received some sort of boon from the goddess Mahaluxmi. The third is the Marathi *varli* which means 'upper' in allusion to the northern situation of the island of Varli in relation to that of Bombay." (da Cunha, p. 58.)

The first of the above explanations is said by more than one Marathi scholar to be untenable as the correct form if the word is to be traced to *vad,* would be *vadali.* The third explanation is said to be the most plausible.

Wyllie Road. *(From Lamington Road to Morland Road.)*

It is near the Adams Wyllie Hospital and was given its name to acknowledge Mrs. Wyllie's generous support of the Hospital named after her husband.

"Mrs. Adams Wyllie came to the assistance of the Municipality when they were sorely perplexed by the influx of famine-stricken immigrants in the year of the great drought, and by bearing the cost of erecting the fine new permanent hospital at Agripada as a memorial to her late husband, she has provided that asylum for the destitute upcountry sick who are constantly attracted by the wealth and philanthropy of this city." (From a leading article in *The Times of India,* July 22nd, 1902, on the occasion of the opening of the hospital.)

Zaoba's Oart. *(A blind lane from Thus Wady.)*

Named after Vishwanath Vithoji Zaoba who bought this field, or oart—then called Ranbil Oart—in the eighteenth century. His great-grandson, Narayen Moroji Zaoba, lives near the oart, which is his family's property. Vishwanath's grandson, Vithoba Zaoba, built a temple of Ram in the locality, which is called Zaoba's temple.

Notes

1. "In the name of Heaven," said Miss Betsey, suddenly, "why Rookery? Do you mean the house, ma'am?" asked my mother "Why Rookery?" said Miss Betsey. "Cookery would have been more to the purpose, if you had had any practical ideas of life, either of you."
"The name was Mr. Copperfield's choice," returned my mother. "When he bought the house, he liked to think that there were rocks about it."
"David Copperfield all over!" cried Miss Betsey. "David Copperfield from head to foot. Calls a house a rookery when there's not a rock near it, and takes the birds on trust, because he sees the nests!"

2. "I am now at Thayetmyo, Mango-Town. And that reminds me how pretty and significant are the names of places in Burma. There are for instances, all the Golden places. Shwele, the Golden Boat, Shwebo, the Golden Mister, Shwegu, the Golden cave, Shwedaung, the hill of gold, Shwelaung, the Golden canoe, Shwenyaungbin, the Golden Banian tree. Then there are all the rocky places—Kyaukse, row of rocks, Kyaukpyu, White rock, Kyaukme, Black rock, Kyaukton, Line of rocks, Kyauktaga, Door of rocks, Kyauktah, Royal rock, Kyaukcho unggyi, Big-stone Stream. There are places named after trees, Maubin, The Man tree, Nya'un glebin, Four Banian Trees, Gyobingo uk, the crooked Gyo Tree, Tant-abing, one Palmyra Tree, Zigon, Plum Hill, Buthidoong, Gourd-fruit Hill, Kyun-gone, Teak hill. Then there are fantastics like Kyatpyin, the Ghost Plateau, Sinmi zwey, the Elephant Tail Pull, Lugaung-gyun, and Human Head Island. With such names places have character, meaning and expression. They are not whittled down to mere colourless sounds as are the names of our towns and villages in England, which require an Etymological Dictionary before they are intelligible. No, the place name in Burma stands out clear and vivid for everyone to understand. And vastly superior they are to the place names of India which are for the most part intended to immortalise the egoism of some complacent and usually insignificant founder. Who cares a plantain for Isa Shah, his

Kot, or Tek Singh, his Toba?" (*Pioneer*, September 17th, 1911).

3. This translation from Balzac was published in *The British Medical Journal*, December 14th, 1912.

4. Adopted to a limited extent in Bombay, e.g., in numbering the cross lanes in Kamatipura.

5. "And the Lord said unto him, Arise, and go into the street which is called Straight, and enquire in the house of Judas for one called Saul of Tansus, for, behold, he prayeth."

6. Liverpool, the birthplace of W. E. Gladstone, has in all nine streets, roads, etc., named after that statesman. London has only two Gladstone thoroughfares, but Manchester and Salford have six Gladstone Streets, besides nine Gladstone Terraces and two Gladstone Villas, and Birmingham has three Gladstone Roads, one Gladstone Street, four Gladstone Terraces, and 11 Gladstone Places.

7. *Bagh* (e.g. Bhattia Bagh). Persian: a garden. Variously spelled baugh, bang, and bag.

    Gullee (e.g. Palki Gullee). Hindustani *gali*, a lane, an alley.

    Khadi (e.g. Umarkhadi). Marathi an arm of the sea, a creek, a deep trench cut to carry off water. Buist's *Guide to Bombay* somewhat narrows down the connotation of the word. "The neighbourhood of the Mazagon Gaol is termed Omarkader, Kader being the word always applied to salt watercreeks dry at ebb tide."

    Moholla (e.g. Vanka Moholla). This is the Persian mahalla, meaning a street, a ward, or a quarter of a town. This Persian word is from the Arabic mahal, a district. (cf. Panch Mahals in Gujarat)

    Oart (e.g. Zaoba's Oart). A coconut garden. The word is peculiar to Western India, and is a corruption of Portuguese orta, now more usually horta. Sir G. Birdwood quoted in Hobson-Jobson, writes: "Any man's particular allotment of coconut trees in the groves at Mahim or Girgaum is spoken of as his oart."

    Pada (e.g. in Agripada) "is identical with the Kanarese padi, meaning a village or settlement, and is one of the many words suggestive of a considerable Dravidian element in the early population of Bombay." (*Bombay City Gazetteer*, I, p. 30)

    Para (e.g. Kamatipura). Sanskrit: a town, a city. In Hindi par, much used in compound words, as Kanhpur—commonly Cawnpore.

    Wada and *Wadi* (e.g. Bhoiwada and Champawadi). Whitworth's *Anglo Indian Dictionary* gives wada, Marathi, from wad, a hedge, an enclosure, a ward or quarter of a town. Wadi, the feminine form of Wada: its use is generally more literal than that of the masculine form.

8. Some valuable notes on Madras place-names in *Vestiges of Old Madras* by Col. H. D. Love (Vol. Ill, p. 560) are accompanied by the remark that "the origin of the present designation of roads and houses within the urban area of Madras is in many cases already forgotten." Lord Carmichael, presiding at the annual meeting of the Calcutta Historical Society in March, 1916, said he wondered whether something could be done to stimulate the interest of members to make individual efforts in original historical research. One point had been brought to his notice, viz., the need of tracing the history of the names of Calcutta streets. Very little was known of Calcutta history between 1785 and 1850. If any members had time to examine the files of old newspapers or periodicals they would probably obtain interesting information about old street names. A recent number of the Society's journal shows that His Excellency's advice has been taken.

9. Today known as Chhatrapati Shivaji Marg—pub.

10. Today it is known as Bombay Samachar Marg—pub.

11. Today known as Sant Tukaram Marg—pub.

12. Today known as Sane Guruji Marg—pub.

13. Today known as Shoorjee Vallabhdas Marg—pub.

14. Today known as Amrit Keshav Naik Marg—pub.

15. Today known as Perin Nariman Street—pub.

16. Today known as Jehangir Behram Road—pub.

17. Today known as Nagar Chowk—pub.

18. Today known as Homi Modi Street—pub.

19. Today known as Veer Savarkar Marg—pub.

20. Today known as Lokmanya Tilak Marg—pub.

21. Today known as Nathibai Thackersey Road—pub.

22. Today known as Sherif Devji Street—pub.

23. Masjid Bunder Road today is renamed as Yusuf Meherali Marg—pub.

24. Today known as Rammohan Roy Marg—pub.

25. Today known as Veer Nariman Marg—pub.

26. Today known as Keshavrao Khadye Marg—pub.

27. Today known as Mahapalika Marg—pub.

28. Today known as N.M. Joshi Marg—pub.

29. Today known as K. Vasudev Balwant Phadke Chowk—pub.

30. Today known as Maulana Azad Marg—pub.

31. Today known as Mahatma Gandhi Marg—pub.
32. Today known as P. D'Mello Marg—pub.
33. Today known as General Bhonsle Marg—pub.
34. Today known as R. S. Nimbkar Marg—pub.
35. Today known as Dr. V. B. Gandhi Marg—pub.
36. Today known as Walchand Hirachand Road—pub.
37. Today Frere Road (part) is renamed as Ganpatrao Kadam Marg—pub.
38. Today known as J. Shankarseth Road—pub.
39. Today known as August Kranti Marg—pub.
40. Today known as M Shuakat Ali Road—pub.
41. Today known as Dr. E. Moses Marg—pub.
42. Today known as Jamnadas Mehta Road—pub.
43. Today known as Pandit Ramabai Marg—pub.
44. Today known as Charanjit Rai Marg—pub.
45. Today known as Dr. Dadabhai Naoroji Marg—pub.
46. Today known as Nayaymurti L. Patkar Marg—pub.
47. Today known as Gadge Maharaj Chowk—pub.
48. Today known as Vithalbai Patel Marg—pub.
49. Today known as Dr. A. Nair Road—pub.
50. Today known as Bhaurao Patil Marg—pub.
51. Today known as Nagindas Master Marg—pub.
52. Today known as Yusuf Meherali Marg—pub.
53. Today known as Jagmohandas Marg—pub.
54. Today known as Mama Permanand Marg—pub.
55. Today known as Syed Abdullah Brelvi Marg—pub.
56. Today known as Dr. Deshmukh Road—pub.
57. Today known as Maharshi Karve Marg—pub.
58. Today known as Khushroo Dubash Marg—pub.
59. Today known as Bal Gangadhar Kher Marg—pub.
60. Today known as S.V. Patel Marg—pub.
61. Today known as Syed Abdullah Brelvi Marg—pub.
62. Today known as Jawjee Dadaji Marg—pub.
63. Today known as Dr. Jaykar Marg—pub.
64. Today known as Sant Savtamali Road—pub.
65. Today known as Bhulabai Desai Road—pub.
66. Today known as Hajarimal Somani Marg—pub.
67. Today known as Senapati Bapat Marg—pub.
68. Today known as Veer Savarkar Marg—pub.

About Indus Source Books

We are a niche, independent publishing house passionately committed to publishing good and relevant literature. Although our primary focus is publishing books on spirituality and philosophy, we also publish general non-fiction in diverse genres. Weseek to provide positive, spiritual insights for harmony and better living. Through our publications we would like to share the received wisdom, lighting the way for fellow-travellers.

We are committed to our goal of promoting understanding of the Self, between faiths and cultures, and of the world in which we live.

Visit our website www.indussource.com for more details.

Indus Source Books
PO Box 6194
Malabar Hill PO
Mumbai 400006
India
www.indussource.com
info@indussource.com